BOB RIEF AND
GEORGE MURGATROYD

AFTER
THE
IDEA

*HOW TO TURN
YOUR IDEA INTO A
BUSINESS*

Flint Hills Publishing

*Flint Hills Publishing
Topeka, Kansas
Tucson, Arizona
www.flinthillspublishing.com

Printed in the U.S.A.

Paperback Book: ISBN 978-1-966323-18-1
Electronic Book: ISBN 978-1-966323-19-8

Library of Congress Control Number: 9781966323181

DISCLAIMER:

While the authors designed and wrote this book to provide accurate and authoritative information with regard to the subject matter covered, they make no representations or warranties to the accuracy or completeness of the contents of this book and specifically disclaim any implied warranties of merchantability or fitness for a particular purpose. Also, while this book may contain general information about legal matters, the information is not legal advice and should not be treated as such. You must not rely on the information in this book as an alternative to legal advice from your attorney or other professional legal services provider. If you have any specific questions about any legal matter, you should consult your attorney or other professional legal services provider. The same applies to financial matters. Consult with an accountant or financial advisor when in doubt or have any questions. Neither the authors nor publisher shall be liable for damages arising herefrom.

The authors have referenced a number of companies. Many of these are companies they have had good experiences with for quite a few years. While they are mentioned, they are not necessarily recommended, except NRI®, because they obviously cannot guarantee you will have the same or similar experience. Likewise, the authors cannot guarantee that by reading this book and applying the information you will have a successful company.

**To our wives Ellen and Tracy
for all they have had to put up with over the years.**

FORWARD

If you are headed for a place you have never been, the best way to get there is to ask someone on the way back!

15.4 percent of people in the U.S. are involved in a startup business one way or another. In 2023 there were 5.47 million new startup applications in the United States. Of these, up to 90 percent will fail, meaning the people who had an idea failed to pull it off and quite likely lost some of their money as well as money from family and friends. *After the Idea* was created to try to change this.

This book consists of a concise checklist laying out sequential steps for those who want to break out on their own and create their own business. *After the Idea* was conceived, designed, and created by those who have already been "there." "There" is a funny place, because there is no "there." It's a state of mind and a practical state of achieving what was first only an idea. Getting there is achieved by nothing short of hard work, sleepless nights, and taking risks when rewards are not guaranteed.

The information in this book did not come easy. We, the authors, come from completely different backgrounds but what we have in common is the desire to help others succeed in business. Here's what author Bob Rief has to say about himself:

> In retrospect, my business life looks like a carefully planned career. That's because you weren't there 5,000 feet underground in the Homestake Gold mine in Deadwood, South Dakota on Christmas of 1964. But I was, and my decision was: *I don't think this is gonna work out for me.* The succeeding years took me

though a career centered on things I liked to do—skiing, hiking, golfing, surfing. Along the way I moved from a product guy to CEO and had the amazing opportunity to work with true visionaries like Georges Salomon, the founder of Salomon® Skis & Boots, or Jerry Lauren from Polo®, Phil Knight from Nike®, Eli Callaway from Callaway Golf, or a few surf visionaries like the Aguirre brothers from Reef® Sandals or Jeff Kelley from Sanuk® Footwear. I learned a few things about myself, and I learned that truly visionary people see opportunity through a different prism. Their steadfast devotion to the idea pushed it through to success, but behind the scenes there is an amazing commonality to the tasks that have to be done to convert **the idea** to reality.

As President of Nike® golf, Bob put together the team that signed Tiger Woods and took that division to great heights. Later he helped take Reef® sandals, Sanuk® shoes, and OTZShoes® to very successful exits.

Today Bob is the Executive Director of San Diego Sports Innovators (SDSI) (www.sdsportinnovators.org) that runs a mentor-led "Business Accelerator" program that supports the sports and active lifestyle industry. The company, founded by the NBA® legend Bill Walton, has matriculated 140 new companies in the last ten years, 78 percent of which remain in business today—an amazing metric considering the national 90 percent failure rate for startups. Additionally, 36 percent of all SDSI graduate companies are female founded.

Author George "Skip" Murgatroyd, brings his extensive legal knowledge to the book. He graduated from UCLA magna cum laude and went on to complete law school in two years at Southwestern University School of Law in Los Angeles graduating with honors. Within two years of graduation, he was made partner at a law firm that he helped grow to national prominence over the next 30 years. He is an AV rated attorney (highest) and listed in Marquis *Who's Who in American Law* and a recent recipient of the Marquis Lifetime Achievement Award. Wanting to try something new, in 2009 he teamed up with the former lead designer at K-Swiss®, the maker of iconic tennis and casual shoes. Together they created

OTZShoes. They asked Bob to join the company who, in a manner of months, took the company to a profitable exit. Skip went on to help create several other start-ups including two where he is currently legal counsel: VIBAe® shoes headquartered in Helsinki, Finland and Gutzi Foods, Inc., a California corporation, which is in the process of making yogurt-based products that are healthier alternatives to several commercially successful products currently on the market.

Virtually millions of ideas die in the ideation stage because the practical task of birthing a new company can be formidable to some. But by reading *After the Idea* and utilizing its checklist, you will walk away with a comprehensive understanding of the critical steps necessary to transform your idea into a successful business. You will be equipped with the knowledge and confidence needed to embark on your entrepreneurial journey with clarity and purpose.

> "The journey of a thousand miles begins
> with a single step."
>
> ~ Lao Tzu

TABLE OF CONTENTS

- ☐ Write out your idea, draw it out, or otherwise get it out so you can look at it.
- ☐ Research existing competitive products and services.
- ☐ Determine viability regarding market recognition & acceptance.
- ☐ Identify and define your customer base.
- ☐ Develop a business plan.
- ☐ Find a mentor.

- ☐ The product process (an overview).
- ☐ Create a protype.
- ☐ Test, collect feedback, & do it again (iterate).
- ☐ Make samples in small quantities.
- ☐ Establish preliminary costs to make your product.
- ☐ Create a preliminary marketing plan.

- ☐ Decide on a name.
- ☐ Check if the business name is available.
- ☐ Create your logo
- ☐ Check if the domain name is available & buy it.

- [ ] Reserve social media platform names including Facebook, Instagram, X, & Bluesky - content comes later.
- [ ] Check if the trademark is available and apply for it.
- [ ] What about a patent?

CHAPTER 4 - SET IT UP LEGALLY   PAGE 53

- [ ] Determine your business location.
- [ ] If there are more owners than just you, agree on ownership percentages & responsibilities up front.
- [ ] Decide upon and set up the legal structure for your business.
- [ ] The shareholder's agreement.
- [ ] The reporting requirements for corporations and LLCs.
- [ ] Tax tip - this is really quite important!

CHAPTER 5 - ASSURE FEASIBILITY & OBTAIN INITIAL FUNDING   PAGE 67

- [ ] Find a manufacturer.
- [ ] Establish margins & know why this is important.
- [ ] Pricing & the value equation.
- [ ] Determine initial funding needs.
- [ ] Initial funding through self, friends, & family.
- [ ] Explore the Minimum Viable Product (MVP) Approach.

- [ ] If you decide to issue stock, you must comply with state and federal (SEC) filing requirements.
- [ ] The Cap Table.

CHAPTER 6 - TELL ITS STORY   PAGE 81

- [ ] Fully develop your story.
- [ ] Create a slogan that helps define your product.
- [ ] Consider/develop a "giving back" associated with your story.
- [ ] Take product shots.
- [ ] Add content to social media platforms.

CHAPTER 7 - MAKE IT LOOK & ACT LIKE A BUSINESS   PAGE 89

- [ ] Create & order business cards.
- [ ] Obtain an EIN (Employer Identification Number).
- [ ] Open two business bank accounts.
- [ ] Finalize your Business Plan with exit strategy & add vision, mission, & position statements.
- [ ] Create a basic website (will launch later).

CHAPTER 8 - PUT A TEAM BEHIND IT   PAGE 97

- [ ] Create your team by defining positions.
- [ ] Set compensation plan & don't forget a stock incentive plan.
- [ ] Set up payroll & payment of taxes.
- [ ] Find a GOOD sales representative.

CHAPTER 13 - LAUNCH IT   PAGE 135

☐ Verify you have the right supplier/manufacturer.

☐ Meet with potential buyers if selling retail.

☐ Advertise pre-sales on your online store.

☐ Go into production on a small scale.

☐ Have a place to store your products.

☐ Have your online store ready to sell.

☐ Create a launch plan and follow it.

☐ Get out there and promote your business/products.

☐ Get products to your buyers.

CHAPTER 14 - GROW IT   PAGE 145

☐ Build momentum.

☐ Arrange for additional finance.

☐ Understand the importance of credit granting practices.

☐ Carry adequate inventory.

☐ Expand your trademarks.

☐ Know the importance of customer service.

☐ Keep getting professional advice.

INTRODUCTION

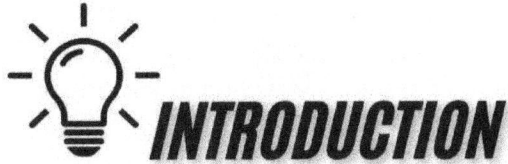

Creativity is flourishing around the world motivated by the spread of ideas—it's universal, it's digital, it's personal, and it's more likely than not, mobile driven. The global pandemic triggered what many have called the biggest event since the industrial revolution or perhaps World War II. Work from home policies liberated many people from corporate drudgery. Working from home created new opportunities for work-life balance, creating time for personal health and recreation. The shutdown of traditional brick and mortar retail accelerated the transition to e-commerce and brought digital literacy to anyone who wanted it: Zoom®, for example. The new workplace allowed many people to see and assess the value of their work in the corporate model. And of course, inevitably, many of us found out that what we were doing for others, we could do ourselves! The genie of creativity is indeed out of the bottle, and it is never going back. This is the time of OPPORTUNITY. The only question remaining is: What are you going to do about it? So, you have an idea? Get on with it! There are no limits, but there are plenty of things to know about how to accelerate your idea from its infancy to reality.

Most people simply do not know what to do "after the idea." This book was developed as a **checklist** to help you turn your idea into a business, and to protect it as well. It doesn't make any difference what kind of business. It can be created to develop and make products, create software and apps, or even a business that provides a service. Most of this information applies equally to all.

The Table of Contents is the checklist. The boxes are there to be checked off as completed. Although we tried to make it a logical sequence of actions, the business world is not that linear. As you will see, some actions under certain circumstances may require you to jump ahead.

The important thing is that the actions get done—not the order in which

17

they are done. This list of actions comes from many, many years of business experience in getting businesses operational, some from the very start and some that were already started and needed help to grow and prosper. Complete the list and you will have a business up and running in short order. If you already have a business, put it through the checklist to make sure you have all the fundamentals covered before it is too late. A business at any stage of development should use our checklist.

Just saying you've started a new business is easy. Running it, growing it, and making it successful is usually far from easy. It inevitably requires hard work and long hours. Nothing is guaranteed, but completing this checklist and following a few of the cardinal rules that follow may help. These are derived from personal experience and learning from those who have failed and those who have been successful.

The Startup Mantra:

1. Be courageous, confident, and focused about yourself and your idea. You are unique. Keep it that way

2. Be practical. Don't quit your day job until you have a viable product that is producing income, or you have sufficient capital to cover your foreseeable expenses. Successful people who followed this rule include Warren Buffett, Oprah Winfrey, and Mark Zuckerberg.

3. Keep overhead to rock bottom minimum—work out of your home or garage. It worked great for Bill Hewlett and David Packard as well as Bill Gates, and for that matter, Phil Knight of Nike® had no trouble selling out of his station wagon either.

4. Keep your supply line short—local if possible. Don't build in China what you could make in China Lake, California.

5. Don't fall in love with your initial iterations. They are going to change. Keep initial inventories very low at the start to allow for change.

ABOVE ALL, FOLLOW YOUR PASSION AND DON'T EVER QUIT IF YOU ARE ON TO SOMETHING!

Co-author Bob Rief once worked for Santiago Aguirre, the founder of Reef® Sandals. Santiago loved to tell the story that as a kid in Argentina he started making sandals from bicycle inner tubes. He luckily found a man who could actually manufacture real sandals which he sold to a few of his Argentinian surf buddies. Then he came to the U.S. but couldn't speak English, so he ended up as a busboy in a Mexican restaurant. Still, he dreamed about his sandals, some of which he brought with him. He would drop them off at local surf shops on Friday and pick up the money on Monday. 20 years later, Bob helped him sell Reef® and he did quite well. A man who stuck with an idea!

Important to Remember

Even if your idea does not work out, the fact that you had an idea means you can have another, and another, until you find the one that does work out. Spend time figuring out what went wrong with an idea and learn from that lesson. This book is designed to minimize the cost of finding that out so you have a chance on the next idea.

As Jeff Bezos, CEO of Amazon®, famously said: "I knew that if I failed, I wouldn't regret that, but I knew the one thing I might regret is not trying."

This is a new era, like nothing entrepreneurs have ever seen before. You no longer must risk everything on your idea. Financing is no longer restricted to your bank account, banks, family, or friends. Financing is now creative and available to all through crowd-funding programs such as Kickstarter® or even Shark Tank®!

One last thing: your motivation should come from your PASSION for creating your product and vision. There will be dark moments when the only thing keeping the idea alive is your absolute dedication; there will be amazing moments when your dream becomes reality.

Good luck and here's to your successful startup business!

- CHAPTER 1 -
PUT YOUR IDEA TO THE TEST

☑ **Write Out Your Idea, Draw It Out, or Otherwise Get It Out So You Can Look at It**.

Got an idea rolling around in your head? Capture it by getting it into a medium that appeals to you. Bring it to life as best you can. Do it now, don't delay—and do not seek perfection!

Today, you can use smartphones that can take notes or dictation, jump on your computer or tablet, grab an ever-present cocktail napkin, or start with a rough sketch on paper. These are the simplest ways to capture your idea on the spot. There is no reason to let a good idea escape. And by just putting the idea down in some form, you can also determine whether it really is a good idea.

Although this will come in much more detail later, laying a basic design or creating a rough prototype would be good at this stage—nothing fancy. Again, the goal is to visualize your idea.

☑ **Research Existing Competitive Products and Services.**

As a preliminary matter, it is important to make sure you are not inventing or bringing to the market something that is already there that **exactly** matches your idea. Luckily, the internet allows for a great deal of research in a very short period of time to answer this question. Try to define your idea the best you can and start your research. See if anyone else is doing what you have thought up. The fact that your idea may be similar to something already on the market doesn't necessarily mean you have to abandon it. The questions become: How is your product/brand/idea different? Is it doing something in a new way? Is it novel or innovative? Does it solve a different problem? What are its features and benefits?

Sit down and make a thorough list that answers these questions. Your list should also include any disadvantages you find along the way. Every market segment has disadvantages, but one universal is your cost and price point compared to competitors.

Another way of going about this is to identify your unique selling proposition (also called unique selling point) or USP. USP is what makes your product or service different and/or better than your competitors. This will become particularly important when it comes time to market your products or services, because your goal may well be to get consumers to switch over to your product or service from what they are currently buying.

To give you a good example, one of the companies that we are familiar with created an aerosol whipped yogurt topping named Yo-Whip® that is a healthier alternative to traditional aerosol whipped cream in that it is made with live and active yogurt cultures and has less fat and calories. As a bonus it also tastes far better. These features easily distinguished it from its competitors.

USP can also include services. Can you provide a service at a lower cost with competitive quality? Or can you add value to an existing product that you are not producing?

You get the idea. Now go tell your USP to friends, family, or someone you respect and see if they are convinced your product or service is different and better. Their feedback may be invaluable in deciding if you want to make any changes or even go forward with what you have created.

We guarantee that it is time well spent, so take your time and do a good job and be honest with yourself.

Also, by doing this you should be able to determine if your product or service is needed or wanted. Believe it or not, it is entirely possible to create something that is not needed or wanted by the consuming public! Teaching a cat to sing sure sounds interesting, but how many people are willing to pay for such a service? An automatic turtle washing station (they get washed as they walk through) sure is a unique idea, but how many people own turtles or even care if their turtles are dirty? You get the idea.

If you give yourself the "green light" remember that you must be all in—no time for doubt!

☑Determine Viability Regarding Market Recognition & Acceptance.

Here's something you may not have thought of—does the public have any knowledge about what your idea has to offer? This is rather a unique issue and one that was brought to our attention by a friend who had a good idea: creating healthy alcoholic beverages. The idea was to create an alcoholic beverage consisting of natural fruit juices to make the drink more "healthy." He raised a bunch of money on the concept alone—to the tune of hundreds of thousands of dollars. He hired a consultant who was renowned for the use of natural juices in soda drinks to develop his product. The two decided they would use Shōchū, a Japanese distilled beverage, as the underlying alcoholic drink that they could add natural juices to create the "healthy alcoholic beverage." They succeeded in creating a prototype that tasted quite good and appeared to lessen a hangover because of its "healthy" properties. When they tried to market it, they ran into a rather large and, what turned out to be, insurmountable problem—very few people had any idea what Shōchū was. They came to the realization that it would take a huge amount of money—more than they could raise—to educate the consuming world about Shōchū. That was the end of that idea and that company.

So, if your idea is so exotic or out of the box that no one has any idea about it, you need to figure out how you are going to educate the consuming public and what it will cost to do so. While it is great be innovative, in the world of business you still must think commercially: Will my product or service have demand, and can I meet that demand and actually turn a profit?

☑ Identify and Define Your Customer Base.

Okay, who is going to buy your product or use your service? While you will be looking into your potential customers in great detail when you write your business and marketing plans (coming up), it's good to have an idea of who they are to begin with. You want to make sure there are enough people out there to keep you in business and can afford your products or services. If your service or product only applies to those who are 100 or older, you are going to have a pretty small customer base!

A good way to start is by:

1. **Defining your ideal consumer:**

    *   Divide the market into segments based on common characteristics.

    *   Include age, gender, location, income, or preference.

    *   Understand the unique needs of each segment and how your product can address them.

2. **Analyzing your competitors:**

    *   Analyze competitors to see who they are targeting.

    *   Identify gaps in their market where your product can offer something unique, better, or less expensive.

Again, you just want an idea at this point.

APPLICATION OF THE ABOVE

So, taking all that has been discussed above and applying it to a real-life company, we give you OTZShoes®, a footwear brand that we helped create and run.

*   What is it?

- o   Minimalist footwear, as natural as possible.

- o   Unique selling principle: cork footbeds.

- What are its advantages?

    - o   Natural resins that fight bacteria and foot odor.

    - o   Natural resiliency, making for a soft, cushioned feeling under your foot.

    - o   Follows the natural contours of your foot.

- Who is the customer?

    - o   Men and women from the Lifestyles of Health and Sustainability community.

    - o   Target age: 30 to 65.

    - o   Global, not local.

- Who are its competitors?

    - o   Birkenstock and Tom's

Based on all these factors we decided to move forward with the company that ended up doing extraordinarily well in acceptance and sales, ultimately resulting in its sale to a multi-billion-dollar conglomerate.

☑ Develop a Basic Business Plan.

Every good business must have a plan from the start—a business plan. A business plan is a document that describes your business, where it intends to go and how it intends to get there. It covers a relatively short period of time—three to five years, sometimes less. It can be basic to complex, depending on what it is needed for and when it is needed. Unless you need it right away to raise funds, at this point it only needs to be basic.

Our research shows a general consensus that a business plan should follow a certain structure, although not always in the following order:

1. Executive Summary

2. Company Summary

3. Products

4. Marketplace Analysis

5. Strategy and Implementation Summary

6. Management Summary

7. Financial Plans

8. Exit Strategy

And don't get us wrong, this structure is not written in stone and there is room for creativity. It is just what is expected. At this point though, you just need it as your road map for your business, so it can be basic and only in fairly-general terms. In a later chapter, we'll flesh it out in more detail because it's the first thing a potential investor will ask for. It is a living rather than a static document in that it can and probably will change as your business grows.

The good news is there are business plans galore to be found on the internet. Just do a search using "sample business plan" or "sample business plan for (X)" where the X is your type of business. Also, there are websites that will help you build one. One we found particularly helpful is BPlans: www.Bplans.com. Here you can view or even download at no cost, existing plans that are broken down to about any kind of business you can think of. There is also LivePlan, at www.liveplan.com, that will walk you through each step of creating a plan and let you edit an existing text to suit your business. But this one comes at a cost—a monthly fee. Why they charge a monthly fee seems silly because it is something you will probably only use once. Maybe they need a new business plan!

The point is that although your business will have unique information, there is no reason to reinvent the format.

If you are selling a product, how you plan to sell your products should be in your business plan. By this we mean which sales channels you will use. Are you going to sell to retail stores known as brick and mortar (also known as business to business or B2B), sell directly to the consumer on the internet (direct to consumer or B2C), or a combination of both?

So, there is:

Business to Business – B2B

Business to Consumer – B2C

B2C plus select retailers.

Say you have a product you want to sell B2B such as REI. That path looks generally like this:

1. Ideation: day 1

2. Prototyping: day 60

3. Manufacturing: day 90

4. Samples: day 120

5. Selling: day 150

6. Retail buys: day 180

7. Retail pays: day 240 (typically 60-day terms)

When you look at it from a cash flow standpoint, you are paying for everything plus additional freight if you are making your products outside the U.S. and then also have to pay for inland transport to a distribution center regardless of where your product is manufactured. So, you have a cash outlay of at least 240 days and then there is the risk at day 300 that the retailer decides the item does not sell and sends them all back!

Throughout this timeline, the retailer is basically in charge of your idea. It is the retailer that tells your story, prices your goods, sells them to its customer base, and proceeds either with a success—which is good for you—or it fails, and you are out of luck.

B2C is the opposite because you are making the product for the consumer, not the retailer. You count on yourself, not the retailer, to tell your story. Your destiny is in your hands. While the process is similar in developmental costs, the difference is in the cash flow. When you sell direct to the consumer, you will be paid at or near the transaction time. The B2C entrepreneur will be flowing cash at least 100 days earlier than B2B, and all risk of storytelling, selling, and returns are greatly reduced. With B2C, you sell through your own site, Amazon®, or both.

Does this mean there is no place for the brick and mortar or the new world brick and click retailer (buying from the retailer's website)? No. Now there is difference. The old model had the retailers calling all the shots and you were at their mercy. Not a good place to be. Nowadays, great retailers find the authentic brands and treat them with respect, not as a commodity that will make them easy money. If your brand is truly authentic and selling, they are coming to you. How do you know when a retailer is someone you can work with? Trust us, you will know!

☑ Find a Mentor.

Do yourself a favor and don't think you know it all or can learn it on the fly. Try to seek professional advice at the start through a mentor. Normally that would NOT be a friend or family member, but rather someone who has "been there." In fact, following the advice of friends and family members is one of the managerial pitfalls that can cause failure. Friends or family can, however, be useful in finding the right mentor. Above all, that mentor should have some knowledge of your product and business and have good management skills.

Most states have helpful programs under the title small business development centers (SBDC). Here's what the one in California has to say:

The SBDC can help you start a business or expand your current business. We offer no-cost/low-cost workshops, one-on-one consultations with business experts at no charge, and assistance with applying for business loans. We can even help you with research, contract agreement review, employee issues, hiring staff, business and/or marketing plan review, and more.

Just do a google search for your state using: "small business development centers" to see if there is one near you.

You can also network locally. For instance, in San Diego there is the San Diego Sports Innovator program (SDSI) created by NBA great Bill Walton and run by your co-author Bob Rief. SDSI is a complete incubator program. Cost? Zero! As stated earlier, the company has an impressive success rate. So, you should definitely check it out if you live in the area.

There is also a company called Score at www.score.org/find-mentor. It offers mentor services regardless of your location: "Score can help you start, grow, or successfully exit a business. Small business owners who receive three or more hours of mentoring report higher revenues and increased growth. Enter your ZIP code to find a free Score business mentor today."

The SBA also has a Mentor-Protégé Program for small businesses. For women there is the Cherie Blair Foundation for Women; for veterans, the Veterans Business Outreach Center (VCOB) Program; and for minorities, the Minority Business Development Agency.

And don't forget to check out Business.USA.gov. There's plenty of help out there to make sure you are on the right track or to get you on the right track with your idea.

- CHAPTER 2 -
CREATE IT

This chapter is geared to those who are creating a product—any kind or type of product—as opposed to a service.

☑ The Product Process (an overview).

Your idea has passed your preliminary considerations, so now it's time to turn it into a product. As you might guess, there is a special manufacturing language that describes the product process:

- Design: all phases of describing the product on paper initially, but soon thereafter, as a prototype.

- Development: your initial effort to bring your concept to 3D life. It almost always includes several iterations of the design. The end goal is a "go to" sample that accurately represents your final design. It's called a "go to" as it will be the reference for the manufacturer whose objective is to duplicate it exactly.

- Commercialization: this involves pattern or tool making or whatever steps it takes to move the product from the development stage into production.

- Production: while this is self-defining, bear in mind that whatever the "go to" sample was, so will be the production, for better or worse. A "sample manufacturing run" is **always** a critical step. Run the fewest number of items the manufacturer will accept. If they are at the quality control (QC) "standard," you can increase to regular runs of large quantities. If they are not right, a small error trumps a larger one.

- Quality Control begins at the beginning, not in post-production. Assessing the "go to" sample, patterns, tools, materials, colors, in the beginning of commercialization is critical. Shakespeare noted: "What begins poorly seldom ends well."

- Transportation: If your product is made offshore you will have to consider the technicalities of shipping. Free on Board or FOB, Ex-Factory, tariff codes, and the like, are all areas of concern. We will cover all in more detail later. Don't be discouraged; freight brokers are experts and are there to help!

☑ Create a Prototype.

This might be the most exciting thing you do if your concept involves making a product. This is the step where you begin to see what "it" is going to actually look like!

The prototype is something that may take a few tries, or many tries (called iterations). Therefore, you should be prudent with the costs involved. In general, we suggest separating prototyping into three phases:

1. "Render" your product in any relevant way to bring it into 3D whether by pencil or Computer-Aided Design (CAD), whatever is easiest for you. You will need to include specifications, dimensions, and thoughts on the manufacturing process. As a note, you need to make sure your manufacturing partner will be able to translate your rendering into a prototype.

2. Assess the materials needed to make a prototype. Remember that the first iteration is simply a 3D rendition of line art. The materials are incidental to the shape.

3. Once you have the material needed, go make the prototype!

One way to start is by creating a digital prototype: You can use various software tools to create a digital representation of your product. If it's a mobile app, try Sketch, Figma, or Adobe XD for designing user interfaces. If it's a physical product, 3-D modelling software like Tinkercad works great.

And really don't worry about the materials. Look around for some that you can repurpose or visit your local hardware store.

If your product involves physical components, 3D printing and rapid prototyping are cost-effective options. Check online to get the best pricing.

For electronic products, a platform such as Arduino is quite good and budget friendly. You can also build a functional prototype by using off-the-shelf components that can be bought online from sites such as electroncomponents.com. Search around to find the best prices.

If you have created a food product, you will probably have to work with a food scientist who can help make the prototype and do the necessary safety analyses. We have worked with a good group in Minnesota called Merlin Development with great success. If you contact them, tell them we say hi!

When looking for guidance, join local or online maker communities and forums. For example, see: forum.makerforums.info. As the old saying goes: "Where there is a will, there is a way." Look around and you should be able to figure out how to make your prototype.

☑ Test, Collect Feedback & Do It Again (iterate).

Once you have your prototype, try showing it around to friends and family to get their feedback. Test your prototype with potential users to gather feedback. Use this feedback to refine your design further. Remember that designing a product is an iterative (repeating) process, and it's crucial to be open to feedback and willing to make improvements along the way. As you refine your prototype, consider factors like aesthetics, functionality, user experience, and manufacturability. The idea is to build upon each earlier version until you get to the point where you are happy with what you have created.

☑ Make Samples in Small Quantities.

Once you are happy with your protype you can turn it into samples. A lot of money can be spent on samples, but it's usually money well spent. You want to get your product right before you show it off to the world. The way to keep the cost down is to sample small amounts at a time. The reasons for this are:

1. Doing one or a few samples at a time lets you iterate on the product design based on feedback and testing. This iterative process helps refine the product, addressing any shortcomings or improving features before scaling up.

2. Producing samples in small quantities allows you to test the market and gather feedback from potential customers. Positive responses can be used to validate the product concept and make data-driven decisions on whether to proceed with larger-scale production.

3. Small-scale sample production allows for better cost control. It minimizes the financial investment required for materials, production, and labor.

With one product one of our companies makes, it took over 62 different formulated samples to find the one that worked best. That was a food product so hopefully your samples will not require such extensive sampling!

So, in summary, producing samples in small amounts is a strategic approach that allows businesses to manage costs, mitigate risks, refine the product, and gather valuable insights before committing to larger-scale production later.

☑ Establish Preliminary Costs to Make Your Product.

Once you are happy with your prototype, you need to get an idea about how much it is going to cost to make your product. As we'll talk about in detail in later chapters, there are many actual costs associated with getting a product to market, But at this point all you really want to determine is whether your product can be made at a cost that will allow it to be saleable and competitive. If you see that your product will cost more to make than a somewhat comparable product already out there, then you need to come up with a different design or even idea. So far you have spent very little money—starting over won't be too painful.

You can get some ballpark numbers by simply identifying components and materials required to manufacture your product. Contact suppliers for price quotes or check online for similar materials.

☑ Create a Preliminary Marketing Plan.

Well, you could start by going to a local university bookstore and poking around in the marketing section! In the absence of you heading off to the campus forthwith, let's give it a shot right now: with the end game in mind, the idea is to create an action plan to achieve certain objectives, an orderly list of actions.

Consider the following example: a ship captain has a cargo, and he intends to deliver it to a specific destination. Christopher Columbus had a destination in mind, but no idea how to get there. He found North America, not India.

Our Captain wants to get to his specific destination. He needs a chart, navigation tools, a crew, a plan to operate the ship, a destination, and estimated arrival date. You are the captain, and you have the same challenges. Your business plan sets out objectives principally from a financial point of view. Your marketing plan is far more operational in nature and tells you and your team what the objective is and sets a measurable path to get there. The benefit of the plan is not just that everyone is on the same ship but that every member of the team has a function to help the ship reach the destination. The marketing plan makes that clear and is essential to good teamwork and success.

Marketing plans come in all sizes and time frames. But time is the enemy of marketing plans. The "fog of war" often scrambles plans, so our suggestion is to start with a simple, several-page document that details out the first 18 months. Plan on evolution and we guarantee you will not be surprised that your initial plan must change.

A good marketing plan has to have certain core elements:

- SWOT Analysis: Marketing professors are cringing, but this single document is one of the most revealing and actionable documents you will produce. Be honest: what are your STRENGTHS, your WEAKNESSES, your OPPORTUN-ITIES, and your THREATS. If you lay them out in a grid and read them backwards, you can make your weaknesses into strengths by taking certain actions; those actions might convert threats into a larger opportunity. That is a damn good marketing plan! More detail on SWOT and an example can be found in Appendix B.

- Target Market and Goals: Define your market channel for goods or services—go back to Chapter 1. By now you should be able to refine your assumptions. Look again and take necessary actions.

- Communications strategy: The marketing director at Google gave us a great tip: if you know who your target consumer is, figure out how they receive information and provide it accordingly. He forgot to add "duh," but we get it! Social media, *The New Your Times*, comic book? Make it your goal to get in touch in the most direct way possible.

- Timeline: This is also important. If you have a destination but no timeline, you may arrive the day after the opportunity disappeared. If you have a plan and you have confidence, apply a timeline and get it done. We admire Guy Kawasaki's admonition in the *Art of the Start*: *The Time-Tested, Battle-Hardened Guide for Anyone Starting Anything*. Start as soon as your product is good enough! If you are an innovator, being first is crucial. You can fix it later.

At this point you probably just need a general plan so you have that map. Marketing is discussed in more detail in Chapter 12. Jump there if you think you need more now.

TM

- CHAPTER 3 -
GIVE IT A NAME

In the world of action sports one of the best examples is Sanuk® Footwear. According to its founder Jeff Kelley:

> "I had an idea for a sandal company, but I wanted it to be different from the crowd and reflect my sense of optimism and humor. I struggled with naming my company even though I had samples in hand. Oddly enough, my neighbor returned from a surf trip to Bali and brought me a gift of a small rock that had 'sanük' laser engraved on it.
>
> 'Sanük? What's it mean?'
>
> He replied, 'It's the Thai word for happiness.'
>
> I looked at the little smiley face the umlaut ü represented, and a light went on: The company name is Sanük® because it means happiness.
>
> It did not stop there: armed with a company name and my first prototype —a sandal made with a astro turf deck (!)—I made my first dealer visit to Jack's in Huntington Beach. I showed the owner the model, this funky green sandal made of of astro turf. He said: 'Are you for real?' That was it—my first model was named—Fur Real!"

Game on!

☑ Decide On a Name.

Now it's time to give your idea a name. Picking a name is one of the more important decisions that must be made at the outset. If your startup is in the service industry, picking a name should not be too difficult. Usually, the name will be the founder's name, such as Craigslist®, or a description of the services to be rendered, like Roto-Rooter®, or combination of location and services such as Malibu local electrician Mark Baysore's business, Ocean Electric.

When it comes to products though, you may have to decide on several names. You need a company name that may not be the same as the name for your product or line of products. Take Levi's® as an example. The company's name is Levi Strauss & Company, and its line of products is called Levi's. On the other hand, Crocs® is both the name of the company and its products. Same goes for Spanx®, Roku®, and Michelin®. So, the question is whether your idea is for just a single product or whether your idea can encompass many products and be a brand.

If your idea is only for a single product, then try giving it a descriptive name that describes its intended use. Here is an example from one of the author's companies. The product is an innovative aerosol whipped yogurt called Yo-Whip®. The name was chosen because it is short, catchy, and easy to remember. It also accurately describes the product, as it is a whipped yogurt that comes in an aerosol can. Additionally, the name is unique and stands out from other whipped yogurt products on the market. Or you can name your product after yourself like Erno Rubik did with Rubik's Cube®.

On the other hand, if your idea encompasses multiple products or a line of products, then you are looking at creating a *brand*. To better understand branding, take a look at the article entitled, "Why Branding is Absolutely Critical for Small Business Success," where business growth specialist Robert Ford writes:

> Simply put, your brand is your promise to your customer. It tells them what they can expect from your products and services, and it differentiates your offering from your competitors'. Your brand is derived from who you are.

In today's global digital market, when you lay down brand values, your customers will hold you to them and judge the brand accordingly. Claim to be a LOHAS company—"lifestyle of health and sustainability?" Then you better be one.

Today's inauthentic brands are called "labels"—they stand for a certain "thing" but nothing additional. Generally, labels represent value in some way, almost always without a consumer reaction one way or the other, in other words, a commodity. Polo® is an amazing brand. Yellow pencils are, well, commodities or *labels*.

Consumers are increasingly well informed. Access to the internet has opened the world to all kinds of brands. In the world of consumer products, an informed consumer will most often choose a brand whose values they share. Something to consider!

☑ Check if the Business Name is Available.

A product name does not also have to be the name of your business. This is true for brand names, too, although less often. If your product name or brand name is also the name of your business, then you want to make sure that the business name is available. Of course, the first place to check is the internet. A thorough google search using your proposed business name as the search term is a good first step. Also check the various social media sites.

It may also be a good idea to spend a few dollars for MyCorporation® to do the search for you. Similarly, a shortcut to this whole process is to use www.directincorporation.com.

This website will let you search for a company name for free, however you must give up your e-mail and telephone number. They will text you the result if you check the box.

Also check with the secretary of state office for your state. For example, in California you can do a business name search by going to:

www.sos.ca.gov/business-programs/bizfile/search-online.

It's great to have a name, so congratulations if yours is available!

☑ Create Your Logo.

The foundation of your brand can be your logo. It communicates your brand. It will find its way to all you are doing including:

1. On the company "door."

2. On all products.

3. On all packaging.

4. On all printed matter; invoices, etc.

5. On your website.

6. On your business cards.

There are volumes written about logos and the development of logos, but chances are you already have an idea of what your logo should look like. If it's possible, the optimum logo represents what your company or product does, or what your brand stands for.

It is also true that some of the best logos are random—they just happen in some meant-to-be way. A great example is the Nike® logo, the famous "swoosh." Nike's Founder, Phil Knight was stumped. He had a brand name, Nike (provided, by the way, by a friend and colleague) but couldn't come up with a logo. He put the challenge to a local art class. Among the many renderings was the *swoosh*. The rest is history. From that came the company's message—"Just Do It!"

But if you get stumped like Phil Knight did, do not despair. There are quite a few people and companies that can help you come up with a good logo—just give it a google search or ask around. Also, you should try out AI image generators such as DALL-E which can be found at ChatGPT, or Midjourney® which requires a subscription. However, if you use either of these image generators you cannot trademark what they create or get a copyright. Both the trademark and copyright offices have ruled that only logos created by a human being can be trademarked or copyrighted! You might find it tempting to play around with one of the new AI image generators. There are quite a few. But if you do so, it should only be for inspiration. If you use an AI-generated image you cannot trademark what they create or get a copyright.

Like business names, many logos do have a rational basis. A good example is the logo for OTZShoes® created by its co-founder Ludo Malmoux. Ludo read an article about Otzi the Iceman, one of the oldest and fully-clothed humans ever found and decided to create a footwear brand around the Otzi story. In addition to having one of the oldest pair of shoes, he had numerous (61 to be exact) tattoos on his body. By combining two of the primary types of tattoos, Ludo created the logo for OTZShoes:

Remember you want your idea or product to be easily identifiable. There are not many people on this planet who don't know that a certain "swooshy" checkmark means Nike.

☑Check if the Domain Name is Available and Buy It.

Let's start with the business name you chose. Your product(s) name will follow the same path. You want people to find your business so a good place to start is with a domain name so you can create a website. A **domain name** is simply a name that's associated with an address on the internet. It is a unique name that no one else can use. Thanks to companies such as Go Daddy® and Ionos®, domain searches are quick and easy. If you go to www.godaddy.com or www.ionos.com, you can type in the name you want to search and get an instant result. Other companies that can do this include Instant Domain Search® and Domain.com.

A word of caution: when you are searching for domain names on company websites that sell domains, be ready to buy! Though there is some disagreement about the practice of "domain front running," we know people who have looked for domain names only to return to find them snatched up and then offered for sale at a higher price. Regardless if this is a common practice or not, if you find the name that you want is available, buy it **NOW**. Don't wait because domain names can go quickly. The cost is minimal. It is best to check each company to see which one works within your budget. Purchasing domain names is money extremely well spent!

In your search you may have stumbled upon what is considered a "premium" name. Almost all three-letter combination domain names that have not already been taken are good examples. If you have absolute confidence in your product and feel wealthy enough then you may consider buying such a name, but more than likely it's time to pick another name that won't break the bank.

It can also happen that if the name you want is already taken, you will be given an option to get the name using a suffix other than .com such as .us or even names like "rocks," "cool," "co," "mobi," "io," "club," or, "guru." While you can take one of these, it is our opinion that you try to find another name that has a .com address available. The reason for this is strictly perception. If you have a .com address you will more than likely be perceived as a legitimate company. It is not that the companies that use these other suffixes are not legitimate, it's just that most consumers are not yet familiar with them and may find them suspect.

Be sure to set up an email account(s) after you secure the domain name. The service you use to obtain your domain name should offer the option to set up an email account using the domain name. For example, you can use your first name followed by the domain name. Or you'll often see "info" or "support" followed by the domain name. This is quite important because it allows you to use your business name in all future communications. It also gives you a jump on Chapter 7 where you will get more information on how to look and act as a business. Never too soon to look professional!

When you apply for the domain name you will be asked if you want help setting up your website. Developing such a site can be expensive, so at this point you just want to have the name. Setting up the website comes later.

☑ Reserve Social Media Platform Names Including, Facebook, Instagram, X, & Bluesky (content comes later).

This is quite simple. Just go to the various websites of the key platforms. Start with a Facebook® page. A search for their business tools page will direct you to where you will find everything you need to know about creating a business page where you can "build an online business profile and get discovered by fans and customers with a Facebook Page." Right now, all you want to do is reserve the name so no one else can take it while you are getting your company together.

Next go to Instagram®. Again, you just want to reserve the name and not create content.

Next is X® (which used to be called Twitter®). Same drill—again just reserving name at this time—content comes later.

And don't forget to investigate one of the newer social media platforms, Bluesky, which as of this writing is growing at a rate of 10-11 new users per second.

☑ Check if the Trademark is Available & Apply for It.

Next you need to see if you can trademark your chosen name, be it business name, product name, or brand name. A trademark protects words, phrases, symbols, or designs identifying the source of the goods or services of one party and distinguishing them from those of others. It is commonly referred to as a "source identifier," the source being your business.

The idea of doing a trademark search may be daunting, but a basic search is not too difficult, although, as will be discussed below, it is not always foolproof.

To do a basic search go to the United States Patent and Trademark office at www.uspto.gov. It used to be easy. Not so much anymore. Now you need an account and go through multifactor authentication. Once through that, the following steps take you through a typical search:

1. USPTO home page (www.uspto.gov).
2. Choose "trademarks" at the top banner.
3. Click on the green box that says Trademark Search System.
4. Type in your word(s) and hit the magnify glass symbol.
5. Next refine your search by goods or services (**see below**).
6. Check Live Box on the left and Registered and Pending.
7. Either a list will come up that you can look through to see if your proposed trademark is taken or it will say "no results found."

GOODS

01-chemicals	18-leather goods
02-paints	19-non-metallic building materials
03-cosmetics & cleaning preparations	20-furniture & articles not otherwise classified
04-lubricants & fuels	21-housewares & glass
05-pharmaceuticals	22-cordage & fibers
06-metal goods	23-yarns & threads
07-machinery	24-fabrics
08-hand tools	25-clothing
09-electrical & scientific apparatus	26-fancy good
10-medical apparatus	27-floor coverings
11-environmental control apparatus	28-toys & sporting goods
12-vehicles	29-meats & processed foods
13-firearms	30-staple foods
14-jewelery	31-natural agricultural products
15-musical instruments	
16-paper goods & printed matter	32-light beverages
	33-wines & spirits
17-rubber goods	34-smokers' articles

The trademark system is divided into different international classes for goods and services. To refine your search, you need to know which class or classes your goods or services fall into. A complete listing of the classes for both goods and services can be found by searching on the United State's trademark website. Scroll down from the introductory paragraph and you will find the Classes with Explanatory Notes. Go through the list until you find the class number that applies to your product. Turn the page to find a chart that has the basic terms for each class to help cut down your search.

It is important to refine your search because the name you want may be taken but is in a different class. Here's an example from one of our footwear companies. We wanted to see if OTZ was available. It was taken. Upon further examination we saw the name in use was restricted to Class 9 (Electrical and Scientific Apparatus). The class for footwear, however, is Class 25, and since Class 9 and Class 25 have nothing to do with one another, the name was available, and we got it.

SERVICES

35-advertising & business

36-insurance & financial

37-construction and repair

38-communication

39-transportation & storage

40-material treatment

41-education & entertainment

42-computer, scientific, & legal

43-hotels & restaurants

44-medical, beauty, & agriculture

45-personal

It is important to know that the fact that your exact trademark does not appear from your search doesn't guarantee you can get the trademark. One of our wives wanted to name her wine company after the piece of property she owned for her vineyard—Jack Rabbit Flats. A search for Jack Rabbit Flats Vineyard resulted in no exact matches. An application was then submitted. Some months later the examiner at the United States Patent and Trademark Office found that there was a conflict with a prior registered trademark —Jack Rabbit Pale Ale. Although there was an argument that beer and wine are entirely different, the USPTO disallowed the trademark because ale and wine are often manufactured by the same entities and fall within the same class.

If this seems confusing or you are not sure of the results of your search, for a relatively small amount of money—usually less than a few hundred dollars—you can have a comprehensive search done professionally by companies such as the Marcaria®. As stated on the Marcaria website:

> Before filing your trademark in USA, it is important that you evaluate possible obstacles that may arise during registration process. Our Trademark Comprehensive Study will not only list similar trademarks (graphic/phonetic) found in the official USA Trademark Database that may conflict with yours but also give you an attorney's opinion about registration possibilities.

Other companies that provide this service are Legal Zoom®, Trademarkia®, and Trademarks 411®.

If at this stage you have great confidence in your product, then you should apply for the trademark now through one of the companies listed above. It may take well over a year to get your trademark approved so the sooner you start the better. The cost is currently $350.00.

The fact that your product is not yet in use does not prevent registration at this point. A statement of use is required but can be filed (for an additional fee of $100) up to six months after the date your trademark is approved. If more time is needed, extensions are allowed at a separate cost.

As a last note, when applying for your trademark you can also include your logo. However, like a name, there may be a conflict with an existing logo and the conflict is not limited to certain classes of goods or services. Even though Nike® products are primarily sports related, if you put a "swoosh" on a soft drink product you are going to be hearing from Nike.

☑ What About a Patent?

Before we start this discussion, it is important to know that patents have a 17-year life span, trademarks are ageless if maintained. The patent for the lubricant WD40 expired about 30 plus years ago, but the trademark ia relentlessly protected. Try getting the trademark using "WD39" or "WD04"—you will be getting a very quick call from WD40's corporate office!

Simply put, a patent protects inventions or discoveries. The United States Patent & Trademark Office describes a patent more precisely:

What is a Patent?

A patent is an intellectual property right granted by the Government of the United States of America to an inventor "to exclude others from making, using, offering for sale, or selling the invention throughout the United States or importing the invention into the United States" for a limited time in exchange for public disclosure of the invention when the patent is granted.

There are three types of patents. **Utility patents** may be granted to anyone who invents or discovers any new and useful process, machine, article of manufacture, or composition of matter, or any new and useful improvement thereof. **Design patents** may be granted to anyone who invents a new, original, and ornamental design for an article of manufacture. **Plant Patents** may be granted to anyone who invents or discovers and asexually reproduces any distinct and new variety of plant.

Patents can also be divided into provisional patents and nonprovisional patents. As stated by the USPTO:

Since June 8, 1995, the United States Patent and Trademark Office (USPTO) has offered inventors the option of filing a provisional application for patent which was designed to provide a lower-cost first patent filing in the United States. But it is important to know that a provisional application for patent has a pendency lasting 12 months from the date the provisional application is filed. **The 12-month pendency period cannot be extended.** Therefore, an applicant who files a provisional application must file a corresponding nonprovisional application for patent (nonprovisional application) during the 12-month pendency period of the provisional application in order to benefit from the earlier filing of the provisional application.

There are additional differences between these patents and the costs vary as well. Also note that a nonprovisional application that was filed more than 12 months after the filing date of the provisional application, but within 14 months after the filing date of the provisional application, may have the benefit of the provisional application restored by filing a grantable petition (including a statement that the delay in filing the nonprovisional application was unintentional and the required petition fee) to restore the benefit.

37 CFR § 1.78 (2014).

The first question is: Do you really need a patent? The answer is: What are you trying to protect? For some businesses, protecting your invention or innovation can make or break your business. For others it may be a big mistake to try to get a patent. The one thing to know about a patent is that prior to approval, it gets published. That's right—it becomes available for all to see. So, if your patent is denied for whatever you have tried to protect, it is now in the public domain.

So it is clear: A provisional patent does not give patent protection. Consider it as a placeholder that gives you an early filing date that is good if you move forward with a nonprovisional patent that is granted. It is a low-cost way of putting down a marker which gives you more time to work up the specifics, test the market, and see if you can afford a nonprovisional patent after a year.

Why is a filing date important? Because in the U.S. (and most other countries) patents are granted to the first to file, not necessarily the first to invent. There have been numerous cases where inventors working independently came up with the same or similar inventions around the same time. This actually has a name—"independent simultaneous invention." These include some of the most important inventions of the last few hundred years such as the telephone, the light bulb, the radio, the microprocessor, and even gene editing (CRISPR).

One thing for sure is that obtaining a patent is an expensive process because it is almost always necessary to use a company or attorney to go through the process. A provisional patent is a lot less expensive and is a good bet if you definitely need a patent but have a limited budget at this early stage.

An internet search will turn up companies and attorneys who can apply for patents. Legal Zoom is one company that we have had success within this area.

An internet search will also bring up dozens of attorneys who practice patent law. Again, make sure you get the costs upfront. We have seen patents run well over $25,000. When determining the costs of these services, look out for phrases like "starting at." It is very important to understand the total costs that you may be getting into. Ideally you want this in writing from whichever company you choose. From our experience, you had better have at least $10,000 set aside for this!

One thing you should do before hiring an attorney is do a preliminary patent search yourself. There are videos on YouTube that show you how to do such a search. Obviously, if the search shows what you were thinking about has already been invented, you do not need to hire an attorney. You just need a new idea.

After you have looked at the other chapters regarding allocating finances, come back to this section to determine how much money you could put toward a patent if you need one.

- CHAPTER 4 -
SET IT UP LEGALLY

It has taken very little money to get this far. Now is the time to fish or cut bait, for rather significant expenses are coming up including the need for professional help to determine which is the best structure for your business. As much as we want to keep things relatively easy to understand, the legal system can be complicated and hard to grasp. So, let's break it down:

☑ Determine Your Business Location.

The easy part first. You need a business location. This means you need an address.

In keeping with the theme of low overhead, try to find a low-cost space. More than a few successful businesses have their roots in a garage, including Amazon, Apple®, Disney®, Google®, and Harley Davidson®. Yvon Chouinard, the founder of Patagonia®, built a small shop in his parents' backyard in Burbank, California, so you're in good company if your business' first address is your home address. Low-rent space other than your home can usually be found if you look hard enough. OTZShoes found an old greenhouse without heat and was frequently covered with dust when the wind blew, but it worked well for the early years. Some states offer programs that include low rent space such as Massachusetts Association of Business Incubators (MABI) which is "an association created for the purpose of increasing support for business incubation programs in Massachusetts, enhancing public awareness, sharing experiences, and exchanging referrals." Check to see if your area has a similar program.

If you rent, it is probably best to avoid long-term leases. This is not just to avoid potential liability should things not go well, but to be able to expand your space quickly should things go extraordinarily well.

You need a base of operation, so do what it takes to find one without breaking the bank.

☑ If There Are More Owners Than Just You, Agree on Ownership Percentages & Responsibilities Up Front.

You should allocate ownership percentages up front. If you will be working with friends or family and think everything will be all right even though your agreements on your business were never put down in writing, think again! If you want your best friend or family member to become your enemy—forget the written agreement and see what happens.

Because you have not yet formalized your business entity at this point, you just want a written outline that allocates ownership percentages, basic individual responsibilities, and things like what happens if one of you die, what if one or more of the owners wants to leave, etc. You get the idea—things you think are important. You want to make sure everyone in your business is on the same page from the get-go. That will save time and potentially money when you get to the next section. So, write it out and have everyone sign and date. This will be incorporated into the business entity you select in the next section.

If you run into an issue on how to allocate ownership interests, take the time to read "The Founders' Pie Calculator" by Frank Demmler. The calculator lists the factors that should be considered and how to assign percentages for each, such as who had the idea, experience, financial contribution, and responsibilities. This calculator is also discussed at www.foundrs.com and is equally worth the read! By playing around with it, you will be given general ranges that you can use as a starting point for discussions.

☑ Decide Upon and Set Up the Legal Structure for Your Business.

There are a number of different types of business entities you can set up for your business. It is imperative to know that there are some very important differences that even some professionals may not be aware of. It all depends on what your long-term plans are for your business, so that should be decided early on because the tax consequences can be significant—maybe we should say, EXTREMELY significant. We have heard some reputable attorneys say that all startups should be limited liability companies, but that could be a huge mistake if you are planning to sell your company in the relative short-term—at least five years after formation. So, if you have already decided how you want to structure your business or have already done so, make sure you read the section below entitled: "This is Really Important!" to make the structure you chose is the right one.

For now, let's go over the choices. They are:

1. Sole Proprietorship

2. Partnerships

3. Corporation (S and Subchapter C)

4. Limited Liability Company (LLC)

Sole Proprietorship

Sole proprietorship simply means owned by one person (while a married couple is obviously two people, they can be considered a sole proprietorship). As defined by the Small Business Administration: "A sole proprietorship is the simplest and most common structure chosen to start a business. It is an unincorporated business owned and run by one individual with no distinction between the business and you, the owner. You are entitled to all profits and are responsible for all your business's debts, losses, and liabilities."

The beauty of a sole proprietorship is that it is created automatically if you do not choose any of the other forms of organization discussed below. A sole proprietorship means it's yours to do with as you please. You are captain of your own ship and chart your own course, but if that ship runs aground, i.e., runs up debt, you are on the hook. From our point of view, probably the biggest drawback is the inability to raise capital. As most entrepreneurs will attest, a successful business needs capital to grow. Unless you are wealthy, this should be one of your main concerns. And then again, if you are wealthy, you have none of the protections offered by the other forms of organization. As a note, a sole proprietorship uses Form 1040 to file its taxes and there is a heightened risk of an IRS audit.

Partnerships

The Small Business Administration has an excellent definition of a partnership. Here's what it says: "A partnership is a single business where two or more people share ownership."

A partnership means more than one person is integral in the decision-making process. This has to be a person(s) that you like—that you can get along with, and who shares a common vision for your business. At the outset you must have detailed discussions on how the company will be run, who is responsible for what, how the profits or any losses are to be split, and everything you can think of that makes you a coordinated team. And here's where you are going to need some money. Everything you have discussed and agreed upon should be reduced to a **partnership agreement** drafted by a competent attorney who will include issues you may not have thought of, such as how to resolve disputes if they ever occur, how to bring in new partners or buyout existing partners, what happens if one dies, or all agree to dissolve the partnership and probably more. Although partnership agreements are not legally required, it cannot be said strongly enough that you should get one. It is extremely risky to operate without this agreement.

Types of Partnerships

There are at least four general types of partnerships:

- **General Partnership (**GP): all partners share equally in the management, profits, and liabilities of the business. Each partner has unlimited personal liability for the debts and obligations of the partnership. If you want unequal distribution, then the percentages assigned to each partner must be set forth in the partnership agreement.

- **Limited Partnership** (LP): has two types of partners—general partners and limited partners. General partners have management authority and personal liability for the partnership's debts and obligations. Limited partners have limited liability (to the extent of each partner's investment percentage) and typically do not participate in the day-to-day management of the business.

- **Limited Liability Partnership** (LLP): like a general partnership but it offers limited liability protection to its partners in that partners are not personally responsible for the negligent acts of other partners. It's typically used by professionals such as accountants, lawyers, and architects.

- **Joint Venture:** a partnership that is formed for a specific project or limited duration. Partners contribute resources, share profits, and usually have shared control over the venture. Some joint ventures can be structured to limit liability, but it is important to note that specific laws and regulations governing joint ventures vary by jurisdiction.

An important term to be familiar with is "flow through." What this means is the profits or losses from a partnership flow through to the partners' personal income tax return reported through a Form K-1. A partnership uses Form 1065 to file its own return although it pays no taxes. That's right—the business pays no taxes. It flows through to the individuals. Also, with a partnership you can have "special allocations" where the profits and losses of the partnership can be allocated between the partners as they like—higher or lower than their actual partnership percentage.

Note: Limited partners and LLP partners are considered "passive investors" which limits their liability to the amount of their investment.

Also, it is worth repeating that limited partners and LLP partners are considered "passive investors" which means their liability is limited to the amount of their investment. For many investors this is of the utmost importance.

Corporations

Next you have the corporation. A corporation is a legal entity created by filing a certificate or articles of incorporation with a particular state's secretary of state office or a similar state agency, and has a legal existence separate and distinct from its owners who are the shareholders.

The first question is which state you should file in? Frankly you will probably need professional help to make this decision. Here are some of the factors to take into account:

1. **Location of Your Business.** You may want to incorporate in the state where your business is physically located. This is typically the most straightforward choice.

2. **Delaware.** Delaware is a popular choice for many corporations particularly those seeking venture capital funding. Delaware has a well-established corporate law system, a specialized court called the Delaware Court of Chancery for corporate disputes, and a business-friendly legal environment.

3. **Nevada**. This state is known for its business-friendly regulations, including no state corporate income tax and strong privacy protections for shareholders.

In summary, look at tax effects, investor preference, and convenience. You can always reincorporate in another state later, but that can be expensive and has its own tax consequences.

Prior to consulting with an attorney or accountant you can research the specific requirements and advantages of each state through their respective secretary of state websites or seek guidance from the Small Business Administration.

There are two types of corporations, the subchapter "S" and the "C." The letters S and C refer to subchapters of the Federal Tax Code.

An S corporation, denoted by its Subchapter S designation from the IRS, begins with filing your business as a corporation. Your corporation will automatically be a C corporation unless you make an election to be an S corporation. To qualify:

- There can be no more than 100 shareholders.

- All shareholders must agree in writing.

- All shareholders must be individuals, estates, certain exempt organizations, or certain trusts. The shareholders must be U.S. citizens or resident aliens. No foreign investors are allowed.

- The corporation can issue has only one class of stock.

- Certain types of businesses, such as banks and insurance companies, cannot make the election.

The key distinction between an S corporation and a traditional C corporation lies in the taxation structure. In an S corporation, profits and losses flow through to the shareholder's personal tax returns, resulting in the business itself not being subject to taxation. However, it is crucial to note that any shareholder **actively** involved in the company must receive "reasonable compensation," meaning they must be paid a fair market value salary. Why is this important? Because you must pay Social Security and Medicare taxes and possibly local taxes on your salary. All money in excess of salary is treated as dividends that are not subject to these taxes. Failure to set a fair market value salary may lead the IRS to reclassify profits that pass through to you as salary and subject all such funds to these taxes along with penalties and interest. You don't want to mess with the

IRS!

In contrast, a C corporation is the conventional corporate structure commonly traded on stock exchanges. It can have an unlimited number of shareholders with no restrictions on their identities. C corporations can issue various classes of stock, including preferred stock. Unlike an S corporation, a C corporation files its own tax return, and this is where a fundamental difference arises.

In a C corporation there is no "flow through" of profits and losses to the individual shareholders. Instead, the corporation is subject to taxation on its earnings and shareholders are taxed on salaries or any distributions. This is known as "double taxation." As an example, if your C corporation earns $100,000 profits in a year and pays out $100,000 as a distribution to its shareholders, the corporation is **first** taxed on its $100,000 profits, and then the shareholders are taxed on any portion of the $100,000 they receive as a distribution. The result is the same money is being taxed twice, hence the term "double taxation."

Regardless of whether it is an S corporation or a C corporation, it must be treated as a distinct entity, and this is paramount. Corporation by-laws demand adherence to specific formalities, including the scheduling of director and shareholders meetings, meticulous record-keeping of meeting minutes, regular updates of the by-laws, stock transfer management, and maintaining thorough records of financial transactions.

As an owner, it's crucial to understand that a corporation is not an extension of yourself—it's a separate entity with its own financial activities. You can't simply establish it and neglect ongoing responsibilities. Each year of operation entails compliance with these requirements. Failure to do so may result in penalties and potentially jeopardize the coveted "liability shield" that corporations provide, thereby undermining a fundamental advantage of incorporating.

When a corporation is first set up it has to declare how many shares it is authorized to issue. A **share** represents a unit of ownership in a corporation and is evidenced by a stock certificate. The certificate is only the evidence or receipt for the shares—it's not the ownership itself.

Usually, a corporation authorizes many more shares than it will ever need—up to 10,000,000 or even 100,000,000 shares. The reason is so that the corporation does not have to authorize more shares later on if needed.

Next, the par value of each share must be declared. Par value is defined as the minimum legal price for which a corporation can issue shares. It is a nominal value assigned to a share of stock and should be set very low—even $0.0001 per share. The par value does not reflect the market value of the stock. The par value can also be set at $0.00 in which case the stock certificate will have the statement "No par value." Here's what a combination of authorization and no par value looks like as imprinted on each stock certificate:

AUTHORIZED: 10,000,000 SHARES COMMON STOCK.
NO PAR VALUE

As a last note, a corporation can issue multiple classes of stock that serve different purposes, such as a preferred class that gives the owner priority in some circumstances. The vast majority of startups will only issue common stock which means all owners are treated the same. If you think you may need different classes, this should be discussed with your legal advisor.

A corporation always has a board of directors elected by the shareholders. Here is where you want talent and experience. While the board is not usually involved in day-to-day activities and decisions, it is responsible for guiding the ship, hiring executives, and overseeing corporate compliance. The board can also create an advisory board that can be crucial for some companies. In fact, we know of at least one company where an advisory board member saved the company. This board should consist of the smartest, most influential, and knowledgeable members that you can get. You may well be surprised by how many people who have been "there" and are now retired and willing to help. In fact, we have found that they find it rewarding and love to share what they have learned over their lifetimes. When issues come up that seem difficult to resolve, they are there to help. Often advisory board members are willing to accept shares of stock in exchange for their services. If you offer shares, be sure to spread the granting of such stock over a number of years. This serves multiple purposes including pretty much guaranteeing their continued service and allowing them to make an 83(b) election. Their accountant should know what this is, but in short:

- The 83(b) election is a provision of the Internal Revenue Code that allows those who receive equity compensation over time to choose to pay taxes on the fair market value of their shares when granted, rather than when they vest, potentially reducing the amount of taxes owed.

- An 83(b) election statement must be filed with the IRS no later than 30 days after the date of the grant in order to receive the potential tax benefits.

Limited Liability Company

The SBA defines a limited liability company ("LLC") as: "…a hybrid type of legal structure that provides the limited liability features of a corporation and the tax efficiencies and operational flexibility of a partnership."

Those that enter into the LLC are known as "members." For all intents and purposes, they own the company like shareholders own a corporation. Depending on the state, the members can be an individual(s), a corporation(s) and/or other LLCs. Members enter into an Operating Agreement, the key document governing the LLC that details how the company will be run. This document allows members to set forth the rights and obligations of members, including their ownership percentage (known as units), how profits or losses will be distributed, voting rights, and how new members can be added or existing members can sell or transfer their units. Members contribute capital (cash, property, or services) to the LLC in exchange for membership units. The value of the contribution often determines the number of units allocated.

Like a partnership, the profits or losses pass through to the members. The LLC pays no federal taxes although it is required to file a separate tax return. It does, however, have a yearly filing fee and may in some jurisdictions be subject to state tax, so it is important to consult with an accountant. As a note, it can also be fairly easily converted into a corporation which may be desirable when raising funds for growth.

When setting up an LLC you must first decide whether the company will be managed by all the members ("member managed") or managed by a manager that may or may not be a member ("manager managed"). If you decide on member managed, then each member has a say in how the business is managed. With a manager-managed LLC, important decisions are made by one person—the manager—who can be a member or non-member. All others are considered passive investors.

A limited liability company can elect to be treated as a S corporation. This election must be made within 75 days of the LLC's formation or by March 15th if operating on a calendar year. If you miss the deadline, you can request late election relief by filing a Form 2553 with an explanation for the delay. The IRS may approve it if the failure was due to "reasonable cause."

One reason you may want to make this election is to reduce your self-employment tax. This is because you can divide business income into salary and distributions. Of course, this is something you must talk to your tax professional about.

There are various companies out there that can help you set up an LLC or a corporation. Our preferred company is Legal Zoom®.

Please remember the above is just an overview. As stated earlier, it is best to consult with both an attorney and a tax professional before making a final decision on which entity is best for your business.

☑ The Shareholders' Agreement.

This is a document that will prevent a lot of potential problems now and in the future. It lays out what shareholders can and cannot do with their shares. **It is imperative that all present and future shareholders sign on to it.** A good shareholders' agreement addresses the situation where all but one shareholder wants to sell their stock in a buyout. That one shareholder could hold up the whole deal and try to get more favorable terms for him or herself by holding out. A shareholders' agreement prevents this by giving the company the right to require that any minority shareholder(s) must sell all of their shares to the proposed offeror on the same terms as all other shareholders. This is called a "drag along option" because any holdouts are dragged along with the majority of the shareholders. It also addresses what would happen if one or more disgruntled shareholders wanted to sell their shares to a competitor. The agreement would prevent this from happening.

A shareholder is one who owns an interest in the corporation, the amount or percentage of which is reflected by the number of shares owned. If a company issues 1,000 shares and you own 100, then you own 10% of the company. In small to medium-sized corporations, shareholders typically get a document called a stock certificate that states the number of shares owned.

A typical recital taken from one of our agreements looks like this:

> The Company and the Shareholders desire to promote their mutual interests by imposing certain restrictions on the sale, transfer, or other disposition of the shares of Common Stock and any other classes of stock of the Company owned by the Shareholders by entering into the agreements contained herein.

The key topics that should be covered in a shareholders' agreement include:

1. Assignability of shares including permitted transfers, no transfers to competitors, first right to purchase, drag along option, and lock up provisions.

2. How disputes between the company and shareholders are resolved.

A sample shareholders' agreement is available by using the QR Code found at the end of this book. Be sure to have yours reviewed by a competent attorney.

☑Reporting Requirements for Corporations & LLCs.

The Corporate Transparency Act, enacted to curb illicit finance, requires most companies doing business in the United States to report information about the individuals who ultimately own or control them.

This applies to new companies as well as those already in existence. Companies created or registered to do business in the United States in 2024 or later **only have 90 calendar days** to file the registration form after receiving actual or public notice that their company's creation or registration is effective. Companies created before 2024 had to file before January 2025. "Companies" include both corporations and LLCs.

Here is the definition of a Beneficial Owner: A beneficial owner is any individual who, directly or indirectly:

• Exercises substantial control over a reporting company, OR

• Owns or controls at least 25 percent of the ownership interests of a reporting company.

An individual might be a beneficial owner through substantial control, ownership interests, or both. Reporting companies are not required to report the reason (i.e., substantial control or ownership interests) that an individual is a beneficial owner. A reporting company can have multiple beneficial owners. For example, a reporting company could have one beneficial owner who exercises substantial control over the reporting company and a few other beneficial owners who own or control at least 25 percent of the ownership interests of the reporting company. A reporting company could have one beneficial owner who *both* exercises substantial control and owns or controls at least 25 percent of the ownership interests of the reporting company. There is no maximum number of beneficial owners who must be reported.

The U.S. Financial Crimes Enforcement Network (FinCEN) expects that every reporting company will be substantially controlled by one or more individuals, and therefore every company, with few exceptions, MUST identify and report at least one beneficial owner to FinCEN.

There are 23 exemptions to this filing although they rarely apply to startups:

Exemption No.	Exemption Short Title
1	Securities reporting issuer
2	Governmental authority
3	Bank
4	Credit union
5	Depository institution holding company
6	Money services business
7	Broker or dealer in securities
8	Securities exchange or clearing agency
9	Other Exchange Act registered entity
10	Investment company or investment adviser
11	Venture capital fund adviser
12	Insurance company
13	State-licensed insurance producer
14	Commodity Exchange Act registered entity
15	Accounting firm
16	Public utility
17	Financial market utility
18	Pooled investment vehicle
19	Tax-exempt entity
20	Entity assisting a tax-exempt entity
21	Large operating company
22	Subsidiary of certain exempt entities
23	Inactive entity

The explanation for each of these can be found at the BOI website you can find in the Resource Sheet. The document that must be filed is called the Beneficial Owners Information Report and can be found there also. The good news is that it is not an annual requirement. The bad news is failing to file this report may subject you to both civil and criminal penalties. Like with the IRS you don't want to miss this filing!

In addition to this federal filing, all states, except Ohio, require some sort of annual report filing. Specific filing requirements and deadlines vary by state, so you have to check with the state where you formed your company. Some states, such as California, also require an initial report when first starting a business. In California it is called Statement of Information and must be filed within ninety days of formation, and every year thereafter. Information about these filings can usually be found at each state's Secretary of State website.

☑Tax Tip – This is Really Quite Important!

There are two important things to know about a startup issuing stock in a C corporation. First, the stock that is initially issued in a C corporation is sometimes referred to as "founders' stock." This is actually a misnomer. The legal term is qualified small business stock or QSBS and those who qualify do not have to be founders.

Under the current law, for stock in a C corporation that was acquired after September 27, 2010 and held for more than five years, there is no tax on the gain on the sale of the stock as long as the assets of the company at time of issuance were less than 50,000,000. The gain is free from income tax, alternative minimum tax, and the current 3.8 percent net investment income tax. Of course, there is always a proviso—actually, two. The excludable gain is limited to the greater of $10 million or 10 times the adjusted basis of the investment. And the corporation must be in a business other than one involving personal services, banking, insurance, financing, leasing, or investing; farming; mining; or operating a hotel, motel, or restaurant.

As you can see, this can make a difference in the amount of taxes you and any of your investors must pay when you sell your business.

The relevant law has gone through a number of amendments in recent years, so be sure to check with your tax advisor.

Second, if one of the founders is only putting in "sweat equity" (no cash—only work), you have to know how to issue those shares without causing serious tax problems. This is known as a "409(a) of the IRS Code problem." Here's basically how it works: Say there are three of you who are starting the company, and each wants to own a third. Two of the three put in $100,000 each to initially fund the company. That means the company has a value of $200,000. If the sweat equity partner is issued one-third of the stock, it now has a value of $66,667 ($200,000 ÷ 3 = $66,667) and is immediately taxable to that person! So, it is clear "stock is not free money." If your company is a C corporation, there are at least four ways around this, but again, you need a tax specialist to explain them to you. If your company is an LLC, there are just one or two. From our collective experience, we can state with absolute certainty that you do not want to mess with the IRS!

- CHAPTER 5 -
ASSURE FEASIBILITY & OBTAIN INITIAL FUNDING

☑ Find a Manufacturer.

If your preliminary cost numbers are looking good, now it is time to find a manufacturer to make sure your product is feasible on a large scale. As much as you may love the idea of making your product in your garage, obviously that will not work on a larger, sustainable scale. So, it's time to look around and see who, where, and even if your product can be made on a commercial basis. You are a company now and need someone to make your product. But first you must protect your idea/product. This is where you are going to need an NDA—Non-Disclosure Agreement. You have probably heard of this before, but if not, go to Appendix C to see what a rather simple one looks like. Basically, it is what it says—an agreement not to disclose what you will need to show to a potential manufacturer. The potential manufacturer agrees to keep your product a secret. This is standard practice, so no reputable manufacturer should refuse to enter into such an agreement. In fact, they probably have one handy that they want to use.

The goal now is to see if it is feasible, both practically and economically, to make your product. To find the right manufacturer is of the utmost importance. Usually this is going to take some time and research. Ideally, you want a company as nearby as possible so you can oversee the process once you are up and running. Of course, this may not be possible, and we have had to resort to manufacturing products all over the world.

Without revealing what your product is, start by asking friends and people who you think may know of any manufacturers that may work. Check with local business development centers, chambers of commerce, or industry associations. They might have recommendations for local manufacturers. No luck there? Then try online. Search online manufacturing directories, like Thomasnet®, Alibaba®, MFG®, and Maker's Row. These directories provide information about various manufacturers and their capabilities. You can also attend trade shows and industry events related to your product. This is an excellent way to meet potential manufacturers face-to-face and evaluate their capabilities.

Okay, here's our checklist:

✓*Check Their Capabilities:* Ensure the manufacturer can produce your product with the required materials, quality, and quantity.

✓*Quality Standards:* Ask about their quality control measures and whether they have relevant certificates proving compliance (e.g., ISO 9001).

✓*References & Reviews:* Request references from past clients and check online reviews. This can provide insights into their reputation and reliability.

✓*Location & Logistics:* Consider the manufacturer's location and how it impacts shipping costs, lead times, and communication.

✓*Request Quotes:* Contact the selected manufacturers and request detailed quotes. Make sure these quotes include production costs, lead times, payment terms, and any other relevant terms.

✓*Negotiate Terms:* After receiving quotes, negotiate terms with your preferred manufacturers. Be prepared to discuss pricing, minimum order quantities, payment terms, and delivery schedules.

✓*Visit the Manufacturer:* If possible, consider visiting the manufacturer's facilities to see their operations firsthand. This can help you assess their capabilities and build trust.

✓*Contracts:* Work with an attorney to draft a manufacturing agreement that outlines all the terms and conditions of the partnership, including quality standards, intellectual property rights, and dispute resolution procedure.

✓*Start Small:* For initial production runs, it's often wise to start with a smaller batch to test the manufacturer's capabilities and quality. This reduces risk if any issues arise.

✓*Build a Relationship:* Maintain open communication with your manufacturer and build a strong working relationship. This can help resolve any issues and ensure the success of your product.

At the risk of repeating ourselves, finding the right manufacturer may take time and effort but it's a crucial step in turning your prototype into a successful product. Remember to perform due diligence, be patient, and seek expert advice if necessary.

☑ Establish Margins & Know Why This Is Important.

Now that you have a workable prototype and a good idea of the cost, it's time to discuss margins, or should I say **MARGINS**—a word that deserves to be bold and in capital letters. This is one thing you really have to know: *margin equals oxygen.* You cannot have too much of it. Your company cannot live without it. It is a critical metric, in fact one of the most critical components of a financial statement. It will be a reference point in most of your conversations with bankers or investors.

There are a few types of margins, like gross margin or profit margin or even the ability to "lever" investments on borrowed money called "margin."

Let's keep it simple. The focus here is gross margin:

The difference between the cost price and selling price of a product.

If you have a $100 of cost in an item and plan to sell it for $150, you have $50 worth of gross margin.

It's a bit trickier to actually *measure* gross margin: Gross margin can be expressed in percent of profit or profit margin:

Percent of Profit:

Cost: $100

Selling price: $150

Profit: $50 (selling price, minus cost)

Percent of profit: 50 percent (Profit divided by *cost*)

Profit Margin:

Cost: $100

Selling price: $150

Profit: $50 (selling price, minus cost)

Margin: (Profit divided by *selling price*) 33 percent

Of the two measurements, the most common usage is the **profit margin calculation**. It's important to stick to one definition. You can see that if you get the two terms confused in a document or presentation, it can have a big impact. There are many profit margin calculators online. Using them will keep confusion to the minimum.

Why does this matter? Because all of your expenses will be subtracted from your margin. The balance left over will be your PROFIT—or lack of it.

So, the practical message here is to know your margin. Before we dig deeper into the abyss of finance, there are a few truisms to be aware of:

- High margin and high volume of sales are *definitely* good.

- Low margin and high volume of sales *may* be good.

- Low margin and low volume of sales means—*no good!* Don't give up your day job, because you are probably going to fail!

Here's an example of why margins are important. OTZShoes came out with a style fairly early in the development of the company which we called the "Moc Shearling." It was a great shoe—a moccasin that looked good, fleece lined, and was extremely warm and comfortable. Pre-orders indicated it was a winner. So, the production was run, in quantity, but we failed to check the margins. After the shoes were delivered and shipped to accounts it was finally determined the style had a negative margin, meaning not only were we making no money on that style (cost was higher than sale price), but were, in essence, actually paying people to buy it!

That's a mistake that you cannot afford to make as a startup. Actually, it's a mistake you can never afford!

☑ Pricing and the Value Equation.

We have chosen to present the complete process here, but bear in mind that not all of these steps are relevant to any one product, since the country of origin is so important. But evaluating each step in the bigger process will give you an idea about how to evaluate your price options.

Here's the checklist:

- **First Cost:** the total cost of the item charged by the manufacturer.

- **Freight Costs:**

○ from the U.S. maker to your specified location such as a distribution center;

○ or FOB (free on board), meaning the goods are shipped from the maker over the rail of the ship, for instance, FOB Hong Kong;

○ or Ex Works, meaning that the freight from the maker to the ship is **not** included, for instance the goods are available in Ex Works Shen Zhen.

- **Duty** (if foreign made): this is a major topic. The short answer is to contact a customs or freight brokerage company. They will help you assess the tariff code and facilitate shipment.

- **Inland transportation,** from the port or point of manufacture to your specified location.

- **The sum of first cost plus all freight, duty, and fees, is your landed cost.** If you decide to produce domestically you will just have a portion of these costs, most likely first cost plus inland transportation to your specified location. Producing anything domestically is much simpler—please do it when you can!

Before you get tangled up in accounting you must have something to account for, namely a product and its price. How much are you going to sell your product for? There are millions of pages on the internet to help you out, but our suggestion is simply to use market prices—that is to say, do some research and make some assumptions.

1. Compare your product. What is it like in the market today?

2. What would the normal consumer of your product *expect* to pay? This is a critical step in the process. The closer the price to the end user's expectation, the quicker your product will sell when it hits the market.

3. Where will your product be sold—internet or brick and mortar retail? One or both? (Discussed in Chapter 1.)

4. If your product will *ever* be sold at brick-and-mortar retail, it will affect your initial price strategy, as the retailer will have to mark it up to sell it. You must plan for that in the beginning. How? Research the market channel. Target a few retailers and ask what their normal markup is.

So, let's get practical and follow an imaginary new revolutionary widget through the process.

1. Product: Double Hinged Alloy Widget

2. Normal single-hinged wire widgets retail for $10.00. Our special double-hinged widget will pull a premium and will sell for $14.00.

3. It will be sold both on the internet and at retail. Widget brick and mortar retailers take a 50 percent margin that means that they will require a wholesale price of $7.00 (retail X 50 percent).

4. Our landed cost in our warehouse is $3.50. Our profit is $3.50 (wholesale minus all cost), so our margin is 50 percent (profit divided by selling cost) if sold at retail.

5. If our sale is on the internet, however, you see our profit jumps from $3.50 to $10.50!

Let's look at a real-world example. When VIBAe shoes was created, the initial idea was to sell **strictly** through its own website, hence the little e in VIBAe for e-commerce. It seemed like a no-brainer because of the great profit difference between selling at retail versus online. The landed cost of one of the models of shoes is $50 and the online price is $150. If you sell to retail, you must sell it to them at $100 because they require a 50 percent margin. Hence you only make $50 a pair at retail versus $100 a pair online. After a year or so it was decided to sell to retailers too. Why not? You get more exposure and add on to your sales. But you want to select the retailers carefully and get them to agree not to sell your shoes on their website or at a price less than what you are selling them for on your website. That needs to be spelled out in your retail agreement.

☑ Determine Initial Funding Needs.

If you are not simply going to sell the idea for your product outright, then you need to get an idea of how much money you will eventually need to get going. It is not that you need the whole amount now, but you need to have a clear picture of where you are now and where you want to go in the future. One thing for sure is that if your idea takes off, you are going to need a lot of funding, but that is covered in a later chapter.

How much money will you need? Start by making a list of all the expenses you think you probably will incur to launch your business. These expenses can be categorized into one-time startup costs and ongoing operational costs. You have already incurred the cost of product development and prototyping, so what else do you need to consider? Some common startup expenses include:

- Legal & professional fees to set up your company—one time.

- Marketing & advertising—continuing.

- Licenses & permits so you are operating legally—periodic renewal.

- Office or workplace rent if you are going to have multiple people to start—continuing.

- Purchase of domain name(s) and trademark(s)—one time although domains require periodic yearly payments.

- Website development with e-commerce if appropriate— initial set up costs with continuing maintenance & updating.

- Insurance—yearly.

- Minimal salary requirements (if hiring)—continuing.

- Utilities and other operational expenses—continuing.

Add up all the one-time costs to determine the total amount you need to get started. Once you've identified all the startup expenses, create a detailed budget that includes estimates for each item. Be conservative with your estimates to ensure you have a financial cushion for unforeseen expenses.

It is probably a good idea to add a contingency to account for unexpected expenses or downturns in business. A common rule of thumb is to set aside 10-20 percent of your total budget as a contingency.

You now have an idea of what it is going to take to get started. If you don't have the money personally, you want to keep the funding simple so as to not run afoul of federal and state regulatory laws on fundraising.

☑ Initial Funding Through Self, Friends, & Family.

In an ideal world you fund the initial costs yourself. But say you can't. So, where are you going to get the money to get this business going? Possibly the best place to turn to initially is friends and family.

Hopefully you have some money to put into your nascent company because when you ask others to help fund your business, they are going to want to know how much you have put into it—how much skin you have in the game. Obviously if they see you are unwilling to invest in your own business, they will be less likely to invest. This doesn't necessarily mean to go out and get a second mortgage on your house, but you should have some monetary contribution.

While some may think it unpleasant or difficult to ask family members or friends for help with financing their new venture, another way to look at this is that it is an opportunity because early investors are those who usually make out the best. Generally, those who get involved in the beginning ultimately get the highest return. In one company we were involved in a few years ago, the early investors saw a return of over 350 percent in less than two years while later investors saw a 50 percent return in less than a year.

Even if your contacts cannot provide actual money, they may be able to provide a service in exchange for a small equity position. Perhaps the most outstanding example of this is the graffiti artist, David Choe, who painted the original Facebook headquarters. You may have heard this story with a happy ending for Choe to the tune of $200 million in stock market float.

One of the founder's' sons of OTZShoes filmed and edited the early marketing videos for the company and in exchange received a small equity position that turned into six figures upon the sale of the company. So, there can be a few things that your business needs that it can get without having to outlay cash.

If friends or family want to put money into your business, it may be a good idea to make it a loan that can later be converted into shares at a set price. If they want equity (which is a share of the corporation reflected by a stock certificate or a LLC Unit) than you need to jump ahead to Chapter 9, "Get More Funding," and determine how much your business is worth so you can establish a share for a corporation or unit price for a LLC.

If family and friends do not come through, you need to explore alternative funding, also found in Chapter 9. Remember in the Introduction we said sometimes you may have to jump around on the checklist. Well, here is where you have to jump ahead.

☑ Explore the Minimum Viable Product (MVP) Approach.

If financing looks like it is going to be an insurmountable barrier, consider the Minimum Viable Product (MVP) approach to minimize initial costs.

Put simply, MVP is a version of the product designed for early customers, offering essential features for usability and gathering feedback to inform future development. You start simple by creating a product with core features that address basic needs/desires of targeted consumers and build on their feedback, so the product is continuously improved. Innovators and entrepreneurs who have used this concept to develop and launch their products include:

- **Dropbox®**– Drew Houston and Arash Ferdowsi used a basic MVP to test their cloud storage and file-sharing idea before building the full product.

- **Airbnb®** – Brian Chesky and Joe Gebbia created a simple website with photos of their apartment and hosted a few guests to validate the concept before scaling Airbnb into a global platform.

- **Zappos®** – Nick Swinmurn initially tested the online shoe retail concept by taking photos of shoes at local stores and only purchasing them from the store if a customer placed an order.

- **Groupon®** – Andrew Mason launched a blog to test the concept of daily deals and coupon discounts.

- **Twitter®** – Jack Dorsey and his team released an early version of Twitter® as an SMS service that allowed people to update their status.

- **Uber®** – Uber's initial MVP was a simple black car service that connected passengers with drivers via a mobile app.

- **Spotify®** – began with a basic MVP focusing on streaming music.

All of these began with the MVP approach to validate their business ideas, minimize risk, and gather valuable user feedback before committing extensive resources to product development. It's a strategy that has proven successful in many industries and continues to be widely adopted by startups and established companies alike.

- CHAPTER 6 -
TELL ITS OWN STORY

Storytelling can be a major factor in building your business or brand. Its goal is to attract and keep your audience. Let them know how things came about and make it interesting.

☑ Fully Develop Your Story.

Every product has a story, even if it's only how the inventor came up with the idea. It is important to get this story to your consumers. It should be relatively short and fun to read. A good example comes from the bike shorts manufacturer Sugoi®: "It all started in 1987 with a sewing machine, a cyclist, a fashion student, and a simple idea: to build a better bike short. From these humble beginnings, SUGOI® was born. And while our garments have evolved, our core philosophy remains the same. We ride. We run. We make the gear that we want to wear. We are passionate about creating the best product—for athletes by athletics—so you can look and perform your best."

This story is really quite good. It tells how the company came about and stresses that it remains true to its core philosophy.

If your product is unique and there is something about it that makes it different or better than your competition, then this should be included in your story. A good example is Yo-Whip® discussed in the prior chapter. It is hands down better than the competitor because it is based on the healthy properties of probiotics found in yogurt and has less fat and calories than traditional whipped cream.

☑ Create a Slogan That Helps Define Your Product.

Every company should have a slogan. A slogan can be a powerful marketing tool that makes your company or product instantly recognizable. A lot has been written about the importance of a good slogan and how to create one. Information on the importance of slogans and examples of good ones can be found in the article carried by *Tripwire Magazine* entitled "50 Examples of Catchy and Creative Slogans" by Dustin Bentonio. (Link found in the reference sheet accessed by the QR code at the back of the book.) Also, we don't think we can write it much better than David Kam at Marketing Deviant put it: "A slogan is a very important element for a brand because it makes it that much easier to increase consumers retention rate and desire. It is an advertising statement that describes what your brand is all about."

Common wisdom about the length of slogans suggests that the fewer the words the better (three to four words if possible). Nike's "Just Do It! ®" is an excellent example. We can proudly use Sanuk as an example—co-author Bob Rief was the CEO of that company. Sanuk created as excellent slogan: "Smile, Pass It On!" The slogan passed on the light-hearted nature of its products—sandals.

Another good example is from the up-and-coming clothing designer DeeDee Deschanel. Until his parents divorced, he was raised in a military family and went to private schools requiring a uniform. Going to public school and being allowed to dress anyway he wanted was quite a shock for him. He found through trial and error that he gained personal strength through choosing the right clothes for him to wear. He carried this lesson to his brand with the slogan, "Strength through fashion."

So, think of something clever that describes who or what your business is and use that as your slogan. If you can't come up with any ideas, there are companies out there that can help. Just google "help with creating a business slogan" and you'll find lots of helpful results. So, you *will* come up with a great slogan—like Nike says—"Just Do It."

☑ Consider/Develop a "Giving Back" Associated with Your Story.

One last thing before you leave this chapter—consider giving something back from money you get from sales. Not only is it good for the brand, but it's good for the cause. TOMS® is probably the best-known company to do this; it resulted in national awareness of the company. For every pair of shoes that was purchased, TOMS gave a pair of new shoes to a child free of charge. While considered ingenious marketing, it had a rather large beneficial effect.

According to Scott Davis, chief growth officer of the brand and marketing company Prophet®, people are more likely to support a company they know is giving back to the community.

It is not a hard thing to do. If possible, it should derive from your story. OTZShoes is a good example. As stated earlier, the footwear brand was modeled after Otzi the Iceman who, it was discovered, suffered from arthritis. His many tattoos are thought to have been a technique used to relieve his arthritis pain. So OTZShoes donated quarterly to the Arthritis Foundation.

This is something you may want to consider at the outset. It's a good thing for your business to do and certainly helps others.

☑ Take Product Shots.

You are about to make your online store operational, but first you need product shots. No point setting up a website without photographs of your products. Obviously, you want your products to look as good as possible, but this does not necessarily mean you have to go out and buy or rent a high-end camera or hire a professional photographer. Of course, if your budget allows for such, you may want to spend some money here. But first you may want to try to use that smart phone you probably have hanging around. There is an excellent article you can find on our Reference Sheet—the webflow.com article—it will take you through the steps of taking high quality product shots at a very low cost. This article explains in detail each step of the process clearly, so in the end you should have some pretty good product shots.

If you don't think you can take the product shots you want, there are companies out there that can do it for you. Good old Google® will find them for you. You can start with a broad search using "product shots" as your search term or be more specific such as "jewelry product shots." You will be amazed how many companies and even individuals there are that are in the business of taking product shots. Of course, like most other services, the cost will vary so you probably want to get a few different estimates. Also, if you have multiple products that you want photographed, you may want to do a test of one or two to make sure you are going to get the quality you have envisioned for your products.

☑ Add Content to Social Media Platforms.

Now that you have a story to tell, it's time to get it out there to the public. There is no better way than through the various social media platforms. Here's how you start getting a buzz about what your business is up to and what to expect. You need this now because, as will be covered in Chapter 8, you may need crowdfunding, and you won't get such funding without a crowd knowing about you. To better understand the importance of social media and crowdfunding, watch the video linked in the reference sheet found via the QR code at the back of the book.

Social media platforms require content. Content can come in many forms, but photographs probably rank at the top. Now that you have your product shots it is time to put them to use. But read on first.

To successfully use social media marketing, you must understand each of them and how they can be used to make your business known and liked. Here's an easy way to differentiate them:

Facebook - "I like coffee."

X - "I'm drinking coffee this morning."

Instagram - "Here's a photo of my favorite coffee."

Pinterest - "My favorite way to make coffee."

YouTube - "Here's a video on how to best brew coffee."

LinkedIn - "I am a barista!"

Now let's go through each of them.

Facebook® – unless you live under a rock, you know it is a social network site that enables companies to create pages for customers to "like," to view company information, and to receive updates through "statuses." Companies can also buy paid advertisements to appear on relevant users "news feeds." The goal is to find new customers and increase sales.

X® – (formerly known as Twitter®) sure has been in the news since Elon Musk took it over. As you probably know, it is a social network site in which users generate 280-character long messages (or up to 25,000 characters for "X Premium" users), called "tweets," to send to their followers. Companies can tweet general information, events, and promotions. It is also a good platform to interact and engage with customers on a more personal level. To successfully use X, you must create or manage your X presence, grow a follower base, drive website clicks or conversations, increase tweet engagements, and find leads through the website.

Instagram® – if you haven't heard of this you must have been sent to a gulag in Siberia. It is a mobile app for sharing and editing photos and videos with a user's followers as well as user's other social media accounts. It provides a huge audience for businesses to creatively engage with their customers. Many businesses use "hashtags" (what used to be called the pound sign or #) to promote their business and start a trend in the community. Your Instagram can also be added to Facebook.

Pinterest® is a website and mobile app that allows users to find, collect, and share their collection of favorite things. Users create virtual "boards" and place "pins" linking to these things often arranged by theme. Pinterest's importance for business is the opportunity to drive traffic to your website while promoting brand recognition.

YouTube® is one of the original video sharing communities on the internet. We can't think of anything better to show you how to do something or tell you about anything! It is the venue for both user-generated and corporate media videos. Many companies have their own YouTube accounts where they post all forms of video advertising to their customers. It is a great way to popularize your product, increase brand visibility, and get feedback from customers. The reference sheet accessible via the QR code has links to several helpful YouTube videos.

LinkedIn® is the business-oriented version of Facebook, mainly used for professional networking. It is a great way to increase brand visibility and credibility. It is also a major platform for recruiting new talent for your company.

Now that you have an idea about what each of these are, you next need to know how to make them interact automatically. Probably the most common automatic interaction is between X and Facebook.

This is the way of the future, it is relatively easy to use and can greatly increase your search optimization which will be explained later, so jump in and have some fun.

BTW, if your idea involves a local business in the service industry or a retail shop, then you have a whole host of platforms that you need to register your business with including:

- ShowMeLocal.com

- Yelp® for Business

- EZLocal.com

- Better Business Bureau

- Bing® Places for Business

- Google® Business Page

- Yahoo®

Okay, you get the idea. There are probably a lot more of these and there is no reason why your company should not be on all of them. This is not time-consuming, and well worth the effort.

To sum up Chapters 3 through 6 using Sanuk® as an example:

- What is the name: Sanuk®

- Domain Name: www.Sanuk.com

- Trademark: Sanuk, Footwear Class 25

- Story: Thai word for happiness, reflected in all Sanuk® products

- Logo: Happy U

- Slogan: Smile - Pass It On!

- CHAPTER 7 -
MAKE IT LOOK & ACT LIKE A BUSINESS

There's an old adage:
"If you are going to run with the big dogs, look like a big dog."

☑ Create and Order Business Cards.

Business cards can do more than just identify the name, address, and telephone number of your business. You can make them an important part of your marketing program that distinguishes your brand from others.

Although the cost of business cards usually goes down with volume, it is best to order small quantities at first. As a business grows it often changes location, requiring new business cards. So, start off with a few hundred at most. You can always order more if you don't move.

There are quite a number of online sites that create business cards including VistaPrint.com, GotPrint.com®, or our personal favorite Moo.com. Having used Moo on multiple occasions, we can say the process is simple, requiring less than 20 minutes to complete.

☑ Obtain an EIN (Employer Identification Number).

Regardless of whether you set up your business as a partnership, LLC, or corporation, you will need to obtain an Employer Identification Number or EIN. You can look at this as the Social Security number for your business. As answered by the IRS on its website:

You need an EIN if you...

- Started a new business;
- Hired or will hire employees, including household employees;
- Opened a bank account that requires an EIN for banking purposes;
- Changed the legal character or ownership of your organization (for example, you incorporate a sole proprietorship or form a partnership);
- Purchased an existing business;
- Created a trust;
- Created a pension plan as a plan administrator;
- Are a foreign person and need an EIN to comply with IRS withholding regulations;
- Are a withholding agent for taxes on non-wage income paid to an alien (such as an individual, a corporation, or a partnership);
- Are a state or local agency;
- Are a federal government or agency;
- Formed a corporation;
- Formed a partnership;
- Administer an estate formed as a result of a person's death;
- Represent an estate that operates a business after the owner's death.

Additionally, you will not be able to open bank accounts for your business without an EIN. Though there are many services that will take your money to "help" you obtain an EIN, this is something we recommend you do yourself. It's not difficult.

Doing it yourself costs you nothing and is really quite simple if you follow these steps:

1. Do a google search to apply for an EIN number online (link in Reference Sheet).

2. At the bottom of the page click on APPLY ONLINE NOW.

3. Then click BEGIN APPLICATION.

4. Go through the steps of the application.

5. Once you complete the application, you are asked to verify it and, once done, you immediately receive your EIN.

Be sure to write your EIN number down in a safe place in addition to printing out the letter from the IRS that gives you the number. This is something you really do not want to lose and a bank is going to want a copy of the letter when you set up your accounts.

☑ Open Two Business Bank Accounts.

Now that you have an EIN it is time to go to your local bank and open two bank accounts for your business. Be sure to take both your EIN and your formal business entity documents such as Articles of Incorporation. You may ask: Why two accounts? Well, this is our recommendation, so you have a checking account for business-related income and expenses and the other a savings account for investment money. It also helps you understand the importance of keeping your finances separate from those of your business.

Note: It is really easy to mix your personal expenses with those of your company but is something that must be avoided at all costs. Your company is not yourself.

While it may be convenient to use your current personal bank, do not. We cannot say it enough! Be sure to check bank fees. You can usually find a bank that waives such fees if you open up both a new business checking and savings account. This incentive can be found by an internet search.

☑ Finalize Your Business Plan with an Exit Strategy and Add Vision, Mission, & Position Statements.

Now it is time to finalize your business plan. In the early days you had an overall idea, but now that idea is developed. While a basic business plan is needed to start, now it needs to be set out in more detail. So, take out your original plan and flesh it out. Put in as much detail as you can.

To further clarify your business purpose and direction, you also need to create the following statements that require a lot less time and effort:

1. Vision Statement: An aspirational description of what an organization would like to achieve or accomplish in the mid-term or long-term future.

This is usually a one-sentence statement that is primarily for internal use, although it can be shared with others. It outlines where you want your business to be in the future. Here are some examples of vision statements:

Amazon®

"Our vision is to be earth's most customer centric company; to build a place where people can come to find and discover anything they might want to buy online."

Amnesty International®

"Amnesty International's vision is of a world in which every person enjoys all of the human rights enshrined in the Universal Declaration of Human Rights and other international human rights instruments."

So, think it through and come up with the vision statement for your business. It's worth it.

2. Mission Statement: A mission statement is a concise written declaration that outlines the purpose, goals, values, and core principles of a business. It serves as a guiding statement that communicates the fundamental reason for the entity's existence and its primary objectives. A well-crafted mission statement helps provide clarity and direction, both internally to employees and stakeholders and externally to customers, clients, and the public.

Whereas your vision statement sets forth where you want your business to be, your mission statement tells what your business is now. For example, take a look at www.kiva.org: "We are a non-profit organization with a mission to connect people through lending to alleviate poverty." This is quite simple with a clear focus.

A mission statement tells a business' customers and employees the purpose of its existence.

3. Positioning Statement: A product position statement will describe how the business distinguishes its products from those of its competitors, how customers can benefit from the products' features, and how these benefits will be promoted to the target market for the products.

Here's a good example provided by Coca-Cola®:

> "Unlike other beverage options, Coca-Cola products inspire happiness and make a positive difference in customers' lives, and the brand is intensely focused on the needs of consumers and customers."

Lastly, and something that is quite important, is the exit strategy. It may seem odd that you need to come up with an exit strategy before you have even begun your business, but it is necessary because quite a few decisions you will soon be making depend on how long you want to keep your business. Are you building the business for the long haul to try and keep it in the family, or do you envision it being sold or even going public and being traded on a stock market? This is something any investors you might end with will want to know. When and how will they realize a return on their investment?

☑ **Create a Basic Website (will launch later).**

The goal now is to just have a basic website in the works. It will probably not be launched until later, once content has been more thoroughly developed. When deciding which platform to use to build your website, determine what type of website you want: informational or online store (e-commerce). Several companies can do either. An internet search using "website builder" or "website builder with eCommerce" should turn them up. Ones that we are familiar with and can recommend include:

1. GoDaddy®

GoDaddy brings to the table all your web-based needs all from the same provider. GoDaddy provides everything from domain names to professional hosting and web development.

GoDaddy is simple to use and requires no knowledge of coding. You start with a blank canvas, and you can drag features anywhere on the page. However, once you choose the theme you want, you cannot change it.

Some other features of GoDaddy include hundreds of design templates, option for custom web design, X and Facebook widgets, 24/7 customer support, ad credits for Google, Bing, and Yahoo.

GoDaddy offers a free trial.

2. Squarespace®

Squarespace has a reputation in the industry for quality. Squarespace is constantly reviewed as one of the best platforms for web design and has become even more useful lately with the release of SQSP20. The beauty of Squarespace is that it provides extensive customization features and requires no specialized knowledge of technology.

Some important features of Squarespace include categorized templates, tablet and mobile optimization, e-commerce features, social media widgets, built in analytics, search engine optimization features, free domain, 24/7 customer support, and unlimited storage and bandwidth.

3. Shopify®

Shopify is also specifically made for e-commerce and one that we highly recommend. Shopify offers a large variety of web themes, all featuring demonstration sites to browse through.

Shopify is simple to use because there is no coding required. You simply choose a theme and adjust features by simple click actions. However, if you do know coding, it allows you to adjust the pre-made coding to make customizations to your site. Some features of Shopify include SEO options, social media widgets, hundreds of customized templates, hosting, and gift card and discount codes.

If you go with Shopify, it will need a lot of product content including product photos and descriptions, costs, etc. This is discussed more thoroughly in Chapter 12.

The good news is that if you have already created a website from another platform, you can add Shopify. Check out our Reference Sheet for the direct link that can help you do that.

IMPORTANT NOTE

No matter which platform you choose, make sure that your website is designed to make it easy for those coming to your site to give you their e-mail addresses. While some people may think it obnoxious that every time they go to a website they are greeted with a pop-up window asking for their e-mail address, it is all for a good purpose. You will learn that there are few things more important in your business than your e-mail list, as discussed in more detail below.

Obtaining a consumer's e-mail requires the consumer's consent which takes us to a final note to make sure your website has a terms of use (also known as terms of service) and, importantly, privacy policy. If you want to use a website, you have to agree to its terms of use which are its rules and guidelines. They are there to protect the interests of both the website owner and the users by clearly outlining the rights, responsibilities, and limitations of each party.

A privacy policy is important in that it is required by many states, and if violated, subjects the owner of the website to significant penalties. The purpose is to inform users of the website what the website intends to do with the users' private information that it may collect at time of purchase. For more, see our Reference Sheet with a link to a good blog post that covers this issue in depth

So, you should go to several of your competitors' websites and see what their terms of use and privacy policies are. They will always be there—usually found at the bottom of the website. You are also free to copy ours at www.aftertheidea.com but we disclaim any liability if you do so. If you have an online store that offers a chat feature, be sure to add an addendum to your privacy policy to specifically address California's statute. An example of one can be found at the bottom of VIBAe's website at www.vibae.com.

- CHAPTER 8 -
PUT A TEAM BEHIND IT

☑ Create Your Team by Defining Positions.

You usually need a team to be successful—small at first but growing as your company grows. The first step is to be honest with yourself. In our un-scientific experience, it's unusual for the founder to also be the "business" guy. As a founder, it could be that your skill set does not include attributes or interest in marketing or other related business functions.

A team is usually put together by first defining responsibilities and positions. A typical organization chart might include these functions:

- design
- development
- manufacturing
- logistics
- accounting
- sales
- customer service
- human resources (can farm out to a company like Bambee HR®)
- distribution

It is not always necessary for you to hire a person for each function, but it is necessary that these very basic functions and related tasks are included in the work plan, and more importantly in the business plan. Our guess right now is that you are thinking something along these lines: *No way I personally can do all of that.*

One alternative to forming a team is to avoid it by licensing your product.

By licensing your product, as opposed to manufacturing it, you can solve a lot of startup challenges. First, you get royalty payments up front without having to outlay any of the cost of manufacturing, all or most of the services listed above are covered, and most importantly, the licensee will have market access and a distribution network. This can free up a founder to focus more of his/her energy on the product itself. The downside to licensing is that you are giving up direct responsibility for the many commercial aspects of your product or brand's future, and of course, the revenue stream is considerably smaller. Many licensing fees fall into 4% to 10% of net sales.

> *I (Bob) learned an interesting lesson from working with Jeff Kelley, the founder of Sanuk®. He started his shoe company with one partner and the part-time support of his wife. He was responsible for not only the design of the shoes but also all marketing and sales activities. It was not long before he realized this was not sustainable, so he brought in a licensing partner who provided him with working capital, provided all the basic business functions, and even paid him a salary. In this way he could focus on design. While he found it hard to give up marketing and selling, he realized it was better than doing all the work himself. As a result, the company entered a period of accelerated growth and a very lucrative exit. All the while, the royalty income was welcome!*

☑ Set Compensation and Don't Forget a Stock Incentive Plan.

An often-asked question by a startup owner is how much salary, if any, should I take? Seems like a fairly simple question, but there are a number of considerations that come into play such as tax and legal consequences as well as the business' financial ability to pay. Again, we send you back to your business plan, to check off your basic decisions about legal and tax consequences. And it's worth noting that if you have decided to take in investors, such as capital partners, you should know in advance that they will prefer that their funds be used to develop the business and not be used for compensation, especially not yours!

Now how do I set the compensation for those who are going to help me—my employees? A well-thought-out compensation strategy is essential for attracting and retaining skilled employees. It's an ongoing process that should be periodically reviewed and adjusted based on market conditions and your company's growth. To start, conduct thorough market research to understand the salary standards for similar positions in your industry and location. Consider factors such as experience, skills, and education levels. Salary surveys, industry reports, and online resources can be valuable in this process.

Some things to take into account include the local cost of living and industry-specific factors that may influence compensation levels. Salaries can vary significantly between different geographic locations and industries. Of course, you must assess your company's financial situation and budget constraints. While you want to offer competitive salaries, it's important to ensure that your compensation structure aligns with your overall financial plan.

You should evaluate the total compensation package, including benefits, bonuses, and any other perks you plan to offer such as special incentives for reaching benchmarks, etc. Sometimes, a comprehensive benefits package can compensate for a salary that may be slightly below market average.

Also, you may want to seek input from your potential hires. Understanding their expectations and needs can help you tailor your compensation packages to attract and retain the right talent.

Lastly, you should strongly consider having a company stock incentive plan—stock set aside for employees, present and future. You want to make sure there is enough incentive to keep or bring talented people into your business. It also makes employees motivated to contribute to the company's growth and success if they have a direct interest in the appreciation of the company's stock. It is probably a good idea to set aside at least 10% and up to 20% of your company's stock for such a plan.

Bear in mind that in many startups, the workload is not full time, at least for many of the functions. The workload for the founder, however, is ongoing and never ending!

☑ Set Up Payroll and Payment of Taxes.

Rule 1: Set aside funds to pay taxes, payroll, and rent in that order. Do not EVER spend money previously set aside for the payment of taxes, payroll, and personnel. Spending the set-aside funds is a recipe for disaster both personally and professionally!

Payroll is a complex process that involves various factors, and accurate management is crucial for businesses to ensure employees are compensated correctly and comply with legal requirements. Here are the key factors that go into payroll:

1. *Wages and salary:* The primary component of payroll includes the regular salary or hourly wages earned by employees.

2. *Overtime:* Additional compensation for hours worked beyond the standard workweek or workday, as mandated by labor laws.

3. *Extra payments* based on performance, sales achievements, or other criteria, which may vary from period to period.

4. *Withholding and remittance* of federal, state, and local income taxes as well as Social Security and Medicare taxes. As an employer you are responsible for deducting these taxes from employees' paychecks.

5. *Deductions:* Deductions for employee benefits such as health insurance, retirement contributions, and other voluntary deductions.

6. *Processing payments* through direct deposit or issuing physical paychecks. This involves coordinating with banks and

financial institutions to ensure timely and accurate payments.

7. *Year-end reporting*: Producing year-end reports such as W-2 forms, summarizing employees' earnings, and deductions for tax purposes.

Did we say complex? Sure is, so we recommend using a payroll service. *Forbes®* has published a good article called "9 Best Payroll Services for Small Business (2024)." You'll find the link in our Reference Sheet.

☑ Find a GOOD Sales Representative.

If you are going to sell to retail, you are going to need GOOD sales reps. While you as founder may be able to cover a number of stores, if you want to grow, you are going to need reps in some or all parts of the country. Obviously, you want to start with the largest market area first and work out from there. If possible, find a rep who is allowed to carry multiple brands because they already have the store contacts.

While you might think that any rep carrying your product is better than not having a rep at all, you may have it wrong. It is actually better to have no rep than to have a bad rep. A bad rep can be a brand killer.

The rep you want is one who believes in your product at least as much as you do as founder. Obviously, you want someone who looks professional, but they do not always have to look the part. If you want a great read, get a copy of *Shoe Dog*, Phil Knight's memoir that documents the ascendancy of Nike®.

As you will find out in the book, one of Phil's early hires was Bob Woodell, a former runner, who was paralyzed from the waist down after an accident and confined to a wheelchair. He did a great job because it's all in the enthusiasm and knowledge of what they are selling.

We collectively have run into about every different kind of sales rep there is, including those who say they can't visit retail stores because they don't want to spend money for gas. There is little doubt that a skilled sales rep is instrumental in driving revenue for your startup if you are selling in the retail space.

Their main job is to acquire new accounts for your brand. Their ability to effectively communicate the value proposition of your startup's products or services can attract and convert potential customers into paying clients who purchase your products on a regular basis.

Not only do reps act as your brand ambassadors, but they also provide valuable feedback on customer preferences, market trends, and competitor activities. This information is critical for the startup so it can adapt and refine its strategies.

The question is: How do you find them? You start by visiting stores and asking managers which reps they like the most and then try to get their contact information. Remember some brands require that the rep only work for their brand, so that is the first thing you want to check. Other avenues include attending relevant industry events such as trade shows or post your job opening on popular online job platforms, such as LinkedIn®, Indeed®, or industry-specific job boards.

You will probably find this is an ongoing process, so always keep on the lookout for good prospects!

- CHAPTER 9 -
GET MORE FUNDING

This is one of the longest chapters in the book. Why? **The number ONE reason a startup fails is lack of money.** Without money you are not going to get very far with your idea no matter how good the idea may be. It is no fun when you run out of cash, so you need to go get it.

There's a lot of money out there for either funding, lending, or investing. Hopefully, this chapter will help you get the money you need to get your startup off the ground.

☑ The Beauty of Crowdfunding.

In the unlikely event you have not heard of crowdfunding, it is the practice of funding a project or venture by raising monetary contributions from a large number of people, typically via the internet. In essence, it is using the internet to raise funds for a specific project, product, or service. This is done through crowdfunding websites that are popping up all the time. Crowdfunding is literally revolutionizing access to capital—move aside bankers, there is a new player in town!

There are three different types of crowdfunding. The first one is where the investor does not receive anything in return other than the joy of helping others. The second is where the investor receives a free or discounted product. The third, and newest, is equity crowdfunding where the contributor actually gets an equity interest in the company.

Let's take the last example first—equity crowdfunding. It's new and it's exciting. Prior to 2015, SEC rules did not allow equity interests to be sold or bought through crowdfunding. That is all changed now. An excellent article to introduce you to crowdfunding is, "What It Is, How It Works, and Popular Websites." You can find the link on the Reference Sheet.

On March 15, 2021, the U.S. Securities and Exchange Commission amended its rules and granted private companies the legal authority to raise up to $5 million within a 12-month timeframe through equity crowdfunding. This method enables fundraising in incremental amounts, accommodating both accredited investors (those meeting specific asset, income, employment, or other criteria) and non-accredited individuals, including family members, friends, and business partners who share optimism about your company's prospects for success.

The revised regulations governing equity crowdfunding are intended to level the playing field for early-stage startups by making more capital available from more types of investors, without the complexities and costs of formally "going public." Our Reference Sheet has a link to a good article on johnstoneclem.com.

Crowdfunding platforms that offer equity crowdfunding include:

- EquityNet®
- Fundable
- LocalStake®
- Republic
- StartEngine®

Of course, the SEC has a say about how equity crowdfunding is conducted. See the Reference Sheet for a link to their position statement.

Here are the basic rules:

- All transactions must take place online through a SEC-registered intermediary, either a broker-dealer or a funding portal.

- Can only raise $5 million in a 12-month period.

- There is a limit on the number of individuals—non-accredited investors—that can invest across all crowdfunding offerings in a 12-month period.

- Disclosure of information must be filed with the SEC, to investors, and the intermediary facilitating the offering.

- Crowdfunding securities generally cannot be resold for one year.

- Crowdfunding offerings are subject to "bad actor" disqualification provisions.

Equity crowdfunding could be a game changer, so check out the sites and see if any are right for your business.

If you don't want to give up equity in your business, or just want to see if you can raise the money you need without giving up equity, you have the other two types of crowdfunding. Here's a list of the more well-known sites:

1. GoFundMe®

2. Indiegogo®

3. Kickstarter®

4. Fundly®

An internet search using the search term "crowdfunding websites" should turn up those that were created since this book was written. To follow the top 10 at any given time you can go to crowdfunding.com. It is updated daily.

But before you adventure into crowdfunding, spend some time learning about it. While it may seem to be an easy source of capital, there is more to it than meets the eye. To set up and run a campaign successfully, we strongly suggest that you read *The Ultimate Guide to Crowdfunding*. You can find the link on our Reference Sheet. You may be surprised by some of the facts/tips that are discussed such as: "Successful campaigns have videos with an average length of **3 minutes-4 seconds**, offer **9 levels of**

rewards, and last for **35 days**." Also, there is no shortage of books on the subject!

☑ Get a Traditional Loan.

Of course, another way to fund your business to get operational is to borrow. Here's where the traditional bank loan comes in. As you probably know, it's not the easiest place to get a loan, particularly when your startup has not made any money yet. But if you have any existing relationship with a bank, it may be a good place to start. If that is not an option, investigate the link on the Reference Sheet to businessloans.com.

Then there are new lending sources that tend to be easier to deal with. These include FundingCircle, and LendingClub (Links on the Reference Sheet). Check them out and see if one will work for you.

☑ Find an Equity Partner.

No doubt you have heard the term VC—venture capitalist—and it means what it says. Venture capitalists are private investors who offer capital to promising business ventures. They typically seek opportunities where achieving at least a 25% annual return within one to five years is feasible. In exchange for their investment, they may require 50% or more ownership to exert control and mitigate the high risks involved. Additionally, they bring valuable management, industry expertise, and business connections. The primary objective of venture capitalists is to guide the business toward its initial public offering (IPO) stage, allowing them to sell their shares to the public at a substantial profit and exit the investment.

If you want to find a venture capitalist, check out the wikiHow link on our Reference Sheet. It takes you through a six-step process to find one.

The VC world is rapidly changing also. There are now alternatives to the traditional VC individuals and companies. There are a number of websites that will find you capital in exchange for equity. For example, investigate MicroVentures®, one of the financial industry's first organizations which merges crowdfunding with the venture capital industry.

Then there are angel investors who provide financial backing for small startups or entrepreneurs. They often offer more favorable terms than a VC and are usually focused on helping the business succeed rather than reaping a huge profit from their investment.

How do you find an angel? Here is a good list to start:

- AngelList®

- Angel Capital Association

- Gust ®

- Life Science Angels

- Tech Coast Angels®

- WeFunder

To learn more about angel investors check out the article on our Reference Sheet that's found at nerdwallet.com. Also ask around in your community. Angel investors usually get their names out because they want to help.

But, if you go the VC or angel investor route, the trick is how to NOT give away too big a piece. If you have ever watched Shark Tank you know what we mean. The panel on the show can like a project or product, but the amount of equity they demand may exceed that which the owner is willing to give up.

So that begs the question—how much do you want to give up in equity and how do you put a price on that? You do that by first putting a value on your business. Well, how much is your business worth? That is not an easy question to answer. In fact, there are no fast and easy answers to this question at all when it comes to a startup that has no track record of profitability. One way of determining the value is to decide how much money your business will need for a set period of time, say one year. Then decide what that is worth to you in terms of percent ownership in the business. If you need $50,000 for the first year and you are willing to give up 25 percent of your business to get this amount, then your business is valued at $200,000. Another way is to find out how much someone is willing to invest. If Mr. VC offers you $50,000 for 50 percent of your business, then your business is valued at $100,000. Another way is to look at what similar businesses have sold for in your industry by going to BizBuySell® or BizQuest®.

As you can see, and as it is often said, "Valuating a startup is an art, not a science." See the link on the Reference Sheet for entrepreneur.com: "How to Value your Startup."

Or: "How to Evaluate a Startup Company" at the link found on the Reference Sheet at dailymba.com.

Or: "How does an early-stage investor value a startup?" See the seedcamp.com link on our Reference Sheet.

And lastly: "How Startup Valuation Works – Measuring a Company's Potential," found on our Reference Sheet: fundersandfounders.com.

No matter how you get to a number, there are two important factors to keep in mind. First try to maintain control of your business by keeping a majority interest (50.1 percent or higher). Second, realize there will probably be multiple rounds of investment as your company grows and needs more money. So do not give up too much in the beginning, if possible.

One last word on funding. Earlier we mentioned Shark Tank. If you haven't seen it, you should. It's on ABC. Its slogan is "Budding entrepreneurs have a shot at making their dreams come true." For past episodes and how to submit your idea or startup go to their website. Yes, the link is on our Reference Sheet.

Nothing ventured, nothing gained!

☑ Check Out Government Loans.

The Small Business Administration (SBA) has a lending program geared towards startup companies. (Link provided in the Reference Sheet.) Although not affiliated with the SBA, this website gives a good synopsis of this program:

> Government small business loans help put your own business within reach. First there's the quest for a decent location, then comes building a customer base, followed by all the initial hiccups of generating a cash flow before your business grows roots and gains momentum. The beginning of a business is crucial because it's when you gain or lose market credibility. If you disappoint your customers, they may not give you a second chance. If your business gets off to a rocky start (most do), and you believe you can recover but need further financing to make this happen, you can apply for government small business loans.

Why Government Loans?

For-profit lenders are reluctant to issue loans to anyone who does not have a strong credit report and financial history that includes earnings. That is not the case with government small business loans. Obviously, a decent credit report is important, and you will have to follow the guidelines regarding the repayment period and the interest rate set by the government, but usually the interest rates charged by government loans are lower than those you could expect in the private sector.

More about Government Small Business Loans.

Government loans are typically offered through banks and credit unions that partner with the Small Business Administration (SBA). The SBA is a U.S. government body, with the motive of providing support for small businesses and entrepreneurs. For each loan authorized, a government-backed guarantee offers serious credibility, since the lender knows that even if you default, the government will pay off the balance.

Different SBA Loans.

The SBA extends financial help through various lending programs it has to offer. For small businesses the best is probably the *7(a) Loan Guarantee Program.* Here's what the SBA says about this program:

"The 7(a) Loan Program, SBA's primary business loan program, provides loan guaranties to lenders that allow them to provide financial help for small businesses with special requirements. 7(a) loans can be used for:

- Acquiring, refinancing, or improving real estate and buildings.
- Short- and long-term working capital.
- Refinancing current business debt.
- Purchasing and installation of machinery and equipment.
- Purchasing furniture, fixtures, and supplies.
- Changes of ownership (complete or partial).
- Multiple purpose loans, including any of the above.

The maximum loan amount for a 7(a) loan is $5 million. Key eligibility factors are based on what the business does to receive its income, its credit history, and where the business operates. Your lender will help you figure out which type of loan is best suited for your needs.

To be eligible for 7(a) loan assistance, businesses must:

- Be an operating business.
- Operate for profit.
- Be located in the U.S.
- Be small under SBA size requirements.
- Not be a type of ineligible business.
- Not be able to obtain the desired credit on reasonable terms from non-federal, non-state, and non-local government sources.
- Be creditworthy and demonstrate a reasonable ability to repay the loan.

The SBA also offers the *504 Fixed Asset Program* featuring fixed-rate and long-term financing. These loans are aimed at applicants whose business model will benefit their community directly, either by providing jobs or bringing needed services to an underserved area. The maximum amount is also $5 million.

There is at least one SBA office in every state in America. If you contact them regarding the startup status of your business model and plan, you can get started on a government small business loan that will give you the financing to make your dreams a reality.

You should also check to see if your state has its own small business funding program. Utah has an excellent one called the Utah Microenterprise Loan Fund. Here is what it has to say:

> Over the past 20 years, the Utah Microenterprise Loan Fund (UMLF) has worked in partnership with members of Utah's financial banking community to help launch or expand more than 800 small businesses across the state.
>
> The UMLF is a non-profit community development financial institution (CDFI) that provides management assistance and loans to new and existing businesses that are not able to qualify for traditional small business loans. Whether loans are used for inventory, equipment, payroll, or other costs, the UMLF understands that small business owners need access to money but often can't qualify for bank loans because they lack a business history, sufficient collateral, or have limited or poor credit.
>
> We're not like a regular bank. For us, lending is about more than making money. It's about helping people increase their incomes, build assets and wealth, feel better about their lives, and build up their neighborhoods. Our application process gives you the opportunity to tell your story, in person, to the people who decide whether to approve your loan. To us, your character is as important as your business plan.

So do a thorough search and see if your state has a similar program. Put in search terms such as "Maryland State funding for small businesses" or

"New York State funding for startup businesses." Play around with these terms and we think you will be pleased with what pops up. You will see that as a small business owner, you are much appreciated. Take New York as an example—small businesses make up 98% of all businesses in that state employing more than half of New York's private sector workforce.

As we said at the beginning of this chapter, there are quite a number of sources for capital these days. Figure out which one is best for you and get on with it. Don't be shy or delay. The idea you have today may someone else's tomorrow.

☑ If You Issue Stock, You Must Comply with State & Federal (SEC) Requirements.

Okay, if you have brought in new investors, and your business is set up as a corporation, you need to issue each of the investors stock certificates that evidence the number of shares they own in the corporation. There are some rules and regulations that you have to follow when you issue stock in a corporation.

First there are state laws. For instance, in California, the corporation must file a Form 25102(f) with the California Department of Corporations within fifteen days of issuing stock to its directors and officers and within fifteen days when issuing stock to any investors on a continuing basis. Be sure to check with your state to see if there is a similar law.

Then there are federal regulations set out by the Security and Exchange Commission (SEC). If you bring in investors and issue them stock, you may have to report this to the SEC—and then again you may not. Because stock issuance is a tricky area, you will need to take any questions you have to your attorney or business advisor. If you want to do some self-education, you can check out the relevant link on the reference sheet provided at the back of the book via the QR code. You'll learn when you need to report stock issuance and when you don't. This is as far as we can take you on this subject. You'll need to work with your advisor to discuss the specifics of your situation.

As a last note, LLCs are not required to report the issue or sale of units to the SEC. However, it is a good idea to see if your state has any regulations on this.

☑ The Cap Table.

A cap table, short for capitalization table, provides a clear and transparent view of who owns what percentage of a company, whether a corporation or an LLC. It is crucial for understanding the ownership distribution among founders, investors, and employees. It lists the equity ownership stakes of all who hold equity in the company.

The reference sheet we provide (accessible from the QR code at the back of the book) lists a good example of a cap table.

To dig deeper into understanding how important a cap table is to a startup, take a look at the article "Capitalization (Cap) Tables Explained: Definition & Examples" by Abi Tyas Tunggal dated June 21, 2023. The link to this can also be found on our reference sheet.

As stated in Tyas's article:

> This essential document provides a comprehensive breakdown of 'who owns what' in a startup, playing a vital role in decision-making for both founders and investors. It serves as a key component in due diligence, illustrating how each stakeholder's equity position shifts in response to fundraising events. As a startup grows, the complexity of its cap table intensifies, making understanding cap table interpretation indispensable for potential investors.

You can create a cap table yourself by using Excel or a similar program or by using a specialized software program found on the internet such as Carta.

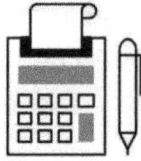

- CHAPTER 10 -
BOOKKEEP IT

While this chapter may be one of the shorter ones, its shortness should not be confused with its importance. It is extremely important to keep track of your finances from the start. You need to know where you are spending your money and where your income is coming from. Once you have that information it is important not to lose it. Here's how you do it.

☑ **Get Bookkeeping Software and Create Chart of Accounts to Track Income & Expenses.**

To start, you need good bookkeeping software for small businesses. QuickBooks® (online or desktop) is probably the best known. The beauty of QuickBooks is that it allows you to quickly generate reports and a lot more. While trying not to sound like a sales rep for the company, here's what you get when you buy their product:

> Free guided setup
> Income and expenses
> Invoice and payments
> Tax deductions
> General reports
> Receipt capture
> Mileage tracking
> Cash flow
> Sales and sales tax
> Estimates
> Contractors
> Connect to sales channels.

But there are a number of other excellent choices that you can check out. These include:

1. Xero® is a highly regarded cloud-based accounting software designed for small businesses. It provides tools for invoicing, expense tracking, bank reconciliation, and collaboration with accountants. Xero® is known for its ease of use and robust mobile app.

2. Freshbooks® is an excellent choice for service-based businesses. It offers features for invoicing, time tracking, expense management, and client communication. FreshBooks is known for its simple, user-friendly design.

3. Zoho Books® is a comprehensive accounting software that includes features for invoicing, expense tracking, bank reconciliation, and inventory management. It integrates seamlessly with other Zoho® applications and is suitable for small businesses of various types.

4. Wave Accounting is a free accounting software that offers basic bookkeeping features, making it a great choice for very small businesses on a tight budget. It provides invoicing, expense tracking, and financial reporting.

5. Sage 50® Cloud Accounting is a more traditional accounting software suitable for small to medium-sized businesses. It offers features like invoicing, expense tracking, and inventory management. Sage is known for its robust capabilities.

All these programs are designed to capture all of your expenses and income so you can readily see whether or not you are making any money.

Once you have this software you need to set up what is called a "chart of accounts." This term is a bit confusing. It is really just categories of income and expenses. A sample chart of accounts for products can be found in Appendix E. By looking at it you will see there are quite a few categories—probably a few you have not thought of before. There may also be a few that do not apply to your business, but not many. A competent bookkeeper familiar with your type of business can normally generate a chart of accounts for you at little expense (less than $100). As your business grows, you may find that you need to expand the categories to make sure all relevant expenses are captured.

As stated earlier, but important to keep in mind—**you need to keep your personal finances separate from your business**. Consider your business as another person. That other person has its own bank accounts, own income, and own expenses that have nothing to do with you. Co-mingling your finances with that of your business can lead to disaster. The way to avoid that is to never do it. Do not lend company money to a friend, do not charge that meal to the company unless it is on company business, do not spend company money on personal items such as clothes, etc. When in doubt, ask your accountant.

☑ Back Up Everything.

Hopefully this section is not necessary because you have already realized the importance of backing up all of your business information. But now that you have created your chart of accounts and hopefully put your financial house in order, backing up becomes essential. We can tell you this from hard experience when we thought the financial information of our company, OTZShoes, was being backed up to the cloud. When the main computer crashed, it must have been a rainy day, because the backup, for whatever reason, could not be found on the cloud. Recreating the business' financial records after that was a nightmare—a nightmare that cost a lot of money and time.

Therefore, we recommend multiple forms of backup. There is the cloud backup. There are multiple companies that offer this service for a monthly charge, including Barracuda® and Carbonite®. There is a good article in PCWorld.com® about how to do this for free. You will find a link to this interesting article aptly entitled, "How to build a bulletproof cloud backup system without spending a dime," by Rick Broida (2013), on our Reference Sheet. The technique he recommends is to back up by type of data rather than by lumping it all together. For instance, documents can be saved in sites such as Dropbox where photos can be saved to SugarSync®. But I'll let him tell you the rest, so take the time to read his article.

Then there is backing up on a separate external hard drive. These are now relatively inexpensive but try not to opt for one that is too cheap. For instance, living by the ocean can cause a less expensive one to corrode (personal experience) and become worthless. Lacie®, My Passport, and Seagate® all have excellent lines that may be worth exploring.

Also, there are simple things you can do for smaller projects and ideas. To give you an example, whenever we completed or made a substantive revision to a chapter of this book, we e-mailed it to ourselves. In this way we had copies available on both of our e-mail accounts which we could access from anywhere, anytime. Works great.

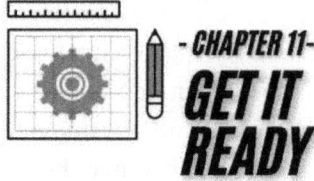

- *CHAPTER 11-*
GET IT READY

☑ Product Test Extensively.

There are not many things more important than testing your product prior to full production. In fact, wear testing is a crucial step in the product development process, offering numerous advantages ranging from improved quality and customer satisfaction to cost savings and enhanced brand reputation. Specifically, wearing testing:

- Uncovers any defects or flaws in your product.

- Helps assess how a product performs under real-world conditions. This is crucial for understanding its durability and longevity in practical use.

- Provides understanding of how a product withstands wear and tear which helps in meeting or exceeding customer expectations. Satisfied customers are more likely to become repeat buyers and brand advocates.

- Gives insight into areas of potential improvement in product design. It allows manufacturers to refine their products for better performance and durability.

- Identifies weaknesses in a product's design or materials early on. It helps to mitigate the risk of product failures, returns, and customer complaints.

- Helps prevent costly post-production recalls or warranty claims. It is more cost-effective to address issues before mass production.

- Provides valuable data for research and development teams, aiding in the innovation of new materials, technologies, and manufacturing processes.

Consistently delivering durable and high-performing products enhances a brand's reputation. Positive reviews and word-of-mouth recommendations can contribute to brand loyalty.

And do not forget to do all the safety tests that may apply to your product(s). For example, at OTZShoes we tested the outsoles of our shoes to make sure they were skid resistant. At Gutzi Foods we tested for shelf life as well as mold growth. You get the idea. Do not let your product go to market without first testing until you know you have your product right and safe!

☑ Create Line Sheets.

More than likely, you are going to need line sheets for sales. A line sheet usually lists each product offering along with a description of the costs, both wholesale and retail. These will be used when making sales calls whether in person or virtual. Our good friend Ludo Malmoux, creative director formerly at Royal Elastics®, K-Swiss, and OTZShoes, and now at VIBAe shoes, has given us permission to use one of the early line sheets for a model that he developed for his new company VIBAe. As the old saying goes: a picture is worth a thousand words. You'll find this example in Appendix D at the back of the book.

In practice, you should develop a line sheet for each different product model.

This will make your and your salespeople's job easier. A line sheet is quite easy to create at very little cost.

☑ Develop Packaging.

Designing good packaging for your company's new products is essential for attracting customers, conveying your brand identity, and protecting the product. Here is a step-by-step guide to help you through the process:

1. Understand Your Product and Audience:

• Begin by thoroughly understanding the product you're packaging. Consider its size, shape, fragility, and special requirements.

• Identify your target audience and their preferences. What appeals to them? What kind of packaging do they find attractive and functional?

2. Define Your Brand Identity:

• Your packaging should reflect your brand identity and values. What message do you want to convey? Make sure your packaging aligns with your brand's colors, logo, and overall aesthetic.

3. Set a Budget:

• Determine how much you can allocate for packaging, design, and production. Your budget will impact the materials and printing options you can choose.

4. Research the Competition:

• Analyze your competitors' packaging. What works for them and what doesn't? Identify gaps or opportunities for differentiation.

5. Choose Packaging Materials:

• Select the appropriate materials for your product. Options include cardboard, plastic, glass, and more. Consider factors like sustainability, durability, and cost.

6. Design the Packaging:

Here you will probably need a professional graphic design firm who will focus on:

• **Visual Appeal:** Use eye-catching visuals, colors, and

typography that resonate with your target audience.

- **Branding:** Ensure your logo and brand name are prominently displayed.

- **Information:** Include essential product information, such as product name, features, usage instructions, and any legal requirements.

- **Imagery:** Consider using product images or illustrations that showcase the product's benefit.

- **Sustainability:** If possible, highlight any eco-friendly aspects of your packaging.

- **Unboxing Experience:** Create an enjoyable unboxing experience that makes customers excited about your product.

7. Choose Printing and Finishing Options:

- Decide on printing techniques like offset, digital, or flexography. Consider finishing options like embossing, foil stamping, or matte/glossy finishes to enhance the packaging's look and feel.

8. Test Prototypes:

- Before mass production, create a few prototypes to ensure the packaging works as intended and fits the product perfectly.

9. Comply with Regulations:

- Ensure that your packaging adheres to all relevant regulations, including labeling, safety, and environmental standards.

10. Get feedback:

- Seek input from a focus group of potential customers to gather feedback on your packaging design.

11. Finalize & Make:

• Make any necessary revisions based on feedback and testing. Once you are satisfied with the design, proceed to mass production.

12. Display Appearance:

• Consider how your products will be displayed in stores or online. The packaging should stand out and communicate the product's value on the shelf or screen.

13. Monitor & Iterate:

• After your product is on the market, monitor customer feedback and sales data. Use this information to make improvements to your packaging in the future.

Remember that packaging design is an ongoing process and it's essential to adapt to changing customer preferences and market trends. Investing in high-quality packaging can help create a positive impression and drive sales for your new products.

☑ Get Barcodes.

Barcodes are required by most if not all retail stores, so if you plan on selling to retail you are going to need them. If you are selling strictly online you can probably pass on this expense.

GS1 is the official provider of bar code numbers; you can find a link to their site on our Reference Sheet. There is also a link to an article, "Ten Steps to Bar Code Implementation" which includes:

• Step 1: Get a GS1 Company Prefix

• Step 2: Assign Numbers

• Step 3: Select a Bar Code printing Method

• Step 4: Select a "Primary" Scanning Environment

- Step 5: Select a Bar Code

- Step 6: Pick a Bar Code Size

- Step 7: Format the Bar Code Text

- Step 8: Pick a Bar Code Color

- Step 9: Pick the Bar Code Placement

- Step 10: Build a Bar Code Quality Plan

☑ Get Insurance.

This can be a bit of a shocker because there are quite a few different types of insurance that you should consider. As you probably know, starting a new product or services company does not come without risks. The risks do vary whether you are performing a service or manufacturing and selling a product. Do not let the following list overwhelm you. Its purpose is to inform you as to what is available. Consult with an experienced insurance broker or agent who can assess your unique situation and recommend a tailored insurance package. Remember that insurance is an essential part of risk management for any business, and having the right coverage can help protect your company's financial stability and reputation.

1.   *General Liability Insurance.* This is a fundamental coverage that protects your business against claims of bodily injury, property damage, and personal injury. It's essential for any business that interacts with customers, vendors, or the public.

2.   *Product Liability Insurance.* If your company manufactures, distributes, or sells products, this insurance can protect you from legal claims arising from product defects or injuries caused by your products. It's crucial for product-based businesses.

3.   *Professional Liability Insurance* (Errors and Omissions Insurance). If your company provides professional services or advice, this insurance can protect you from claims of negligence, errors, or omissions in your services. It's common for consulting firms or

businesses that offer specialized expertise.

4.   *Property Insurance.* This coverage protects your physical assets, including your office space, equipment, inventory, and other business property from events like fire, theft, or natural disasters.

5.   *Business Interruption Insurance.* This insurance helps cover lost income and ongoing expenses if your business is temporarily unable to operate due to a covered event, such as a fire or natural disaster.

6.   *Commercial Auto Insurance.* If your company uses vehicles for business purposes, you'll need commercial auto insurance to protect your vehicles and drivers in case of accidents.

7.   *Workers' Compensation Insurance.* If you have employees, workers' comp insurance is typically required by law. It provides coverage for medical expenses and lost wages if an employee is injured on the job.

8.   *Cybersecurity Insurance.* In an increasingly digital world, this insurance helps protect your business from losses resulting from data breaches, cyberattacks, or other technology-related issues.

9.   *Product Recall Insurance.* If you manufacture or sell products, this insurance can help cover the costs associated with a product recall due to safety concerns or defects.

10.   *Commercial Umbrella Insurance.* This policy provides additional liability coverage beyond the limits of your primary liability policies, offering extra protection in case of major lawsuits or claims.

11.   *Directors and Officers Insurance (D & O).* If your company has a board of directors or officers, D&O insurance can protect them from personal liability in case of legal actions related to their decisions and actions in managing the company.

12.   *Employment Practices Liability Insurance.* This insurance

helps protect your business against claims of wrongful employment practices, such as discrimination, harassment, or wrongful termination.

Now you know why you have probably never met a poor insurance agent!

☑ Get Required Licenses & Permits.

Here's where the regulatory part comes in. What isn't regulated these days? Well, businesses are certainly regulated, and you don't want to run afoul of federal, state, or local agencies. So, what do you need to do? Well, you are already covered on the federal level when you got your EIN. Now you have to deal with the state and local regulations. Telling you what the requirements and specific regulations for every city, county, or state is well beyond the capability of this book. We can however, tell you generally what you need to look out for and obtain.

First there is the business license. This is not to be confused with permits which are discussed below. Whether you are running an online retail business or a brick-and-mortar retail store, you are probably going to need a business license. Most if not all service businesses also need a business license. Typically, they are the same.

Then there are the seller's permit and resale certificate. Some states merge these two into one. The seller's permit is issued by the state and means that you will be collecting sales tax on behalf of the state. You are an identified collector of sales tax.

A resale certificate allows you to buy goods at the wholesale level without having to pay sales tax. This only applies if you are buying the goods with the intention of later re-selling them. These include wholesale items for resale and items that are purchased for use in the manufacture of products for resale. Your resale certificate allows the seller to avoid paying the sales tax. For example, if you are in the T-shirt retail business that has various designs, you buy your blank T-shirts wholesale and do not pay any tax. Once you put your design on the T-shirts and sell them you must collect tax on those sales. That's what is referred to as the resale.

If this seems confusing at all, an excellent article on permits and resale certificates can be found on our Reference Sheet.

Remember that licensing requirements and regulations vary, so be sure to research what your state requires.

- CHAPTER 12 -
MARKET IT

☑ More on Marketing.

Marketing is critical, so we are going to be a bit repetitive and give you a comprehensive overview of a simple and effective marketing plan for a startup company that you can use as a checklist:

✓ *Define Your Target Audience.* Start by identifying your ideal customers. Consider demographics, psychographics, and their buying behavior. This will help tailor your marketing efforts effectively.

✓ *Create a Unique Value Proposition* (UVP). Determine what sets your retail business apart from competitors. Your UVP should communicate the unique benefits customers will receive from your products or services.

✓ *Build a Strong Online Presence.* In today's digital age, having an online presence is crucial. Create a professional website and set up social media profiles on platforms your target audience frequents.

✓ *Content Marketing.* Develop valuable and relevant content that resonates with your audience. This could include blog posts, videos, infographics, or how-to guides related to your products or industry.

✓ *Email Marketing.* Build an email list of interested customers and send out regular newsletters with promotions, product updates, and valuable content. Consider using free or low-cost email marketing platforms.

✓ *Leverage Social Media.* Use social media to engage with your audience. Share product updates, behind-the-scenes content, customer testimonials, and run targeted ads to reach potential customers.

✓ *Local SEO (Search Engine Optimization).* Optimize your website for local search by including location-based keywords in your content and meta descriptions. Claim and update your "Google My Business" listing.

✓ *Partnerships & Collaborations.* Partner with local businesses or influencers in your niche for co-promotions and cross-marketing opportunities. This can help you tap into their established audience.

✓ *Customer Loyalty Program.* Reward repeat customers with a loyalty program. This can be as simple as offering discounts or freebies for frequent purchases.

✓ *Measure & Adjust.* Use free or affordable analytics tools to track your marketing efforts. Monitor website traffic, email open rates, social media engagement, and sales. Adjust your strategy based on what works best.

✓ *Guerilla Marketing.* Get creative with low-cost, unconventional marketing tactics like sidewalk chalk art, hosting pop-up shops, or participating in local events and fairs.

✓ *Word-of-Mouth Marketing.* Encourage satisfied customers to refer friends and family to your business by offering incentives or discounts for referrals.

✓ *Create a contest.* Reading and follow the advice of Denise Wakeman. You can find her article on our Reference Sheet.

✓ *Online Reviews & Reputation Management.* Encourage customers to leave reviews on platforms like Google, Yelp, or

Trustpilot. Respond to reviews, both positive and negative, professionally and promptly.

✓ *Budget Wisely.* Keep a close eye on your marketing budget. Allocate funds to strategies that provide the best return on investment.

✓*Learn from Competitors.* Study what successful competitors are doing in terms of marketing and adapt their strategies to your business, making improvements where needed. Remember that consistency is key in marketing. It may take time to see significant results, but by implementing these low-cost strategies and continuously refining your approach, your retail startup can build a strong brand and customer base without breaking the bank. See the article from coresignal.com; link provided on our Reference Sheet.

In this age of AI, there are websites that can help you with marketing. GoDaddy recently created just such a tool. It is called Airo and can be found at their site (see our Reference Sheet). We highly recommend that you take the time to go through all the material on this site thoroughly. Also search the web for other such sites. Good marketing can make or break a start-up!

We should mention here that most if not all the following steps can be done by a good public relations firm. Here is where your budget comes in. A good PR firm will not come cheap, and in addition to an upfront fee, there may well be a monthly retainer. However, if you have the money, it is well worth it because not only will each of the following actions get done right and professionally, but it will also free you up to do the myriad other things needed to launch, as set forth below.

☑ Turn Your Product Shots into a LookBook.

Look Book or LookBook may be a new term to you. One definition is a set of photographs displaying a fashion designer's new collection, assembled for marketing purposes. But products other than those created by a fashion designer should have a LookBook. For examples see the article on Design Shack on our Reference Sheet.

A LookBook is basically a book of photographs that show the look of your product as it is intended to be used. If it's clothing, then have a person wearing the clothes—preferably someone who is a target consumer. If it's a useful product, show someone using it. You get the idea.

A LookBook is different from product shots. It is different from a catalog in that it does not include prices. It is not a line sheet either. But of course, you are free to make yours any way you want. The bottom line is you want to make people feel excited about your products, you want to arouse their interest, you want them to start a conversation or find out more about you.

Like your product shots, you can try and do these yourself or bring in someone to help you.

Once you have the shots, you have to create the book. There are quite a few companies out there that will take your photographs and bind them into a fine-looking book. A good example is Flipsnack®. You'll find a link on our Reference Sheet that lists seven worth looking into.

An alternative is to create a digital LookBook. You can put all of your photographs on a USB (kind of old now) or the newer USB-Type C thumb drive to hand out to potential customers.

Also, it is a good idea to put it on your website. But remember, the photos have to be good. As an old friend once made clear: "You only get one chance to make a good first impression."

☑ Make Sure Your Website is Optimized.

Here's a term you don't want to forget—SEO or search engine optimization. That term has been around for quite a while now and some think it may be dead. Others think it is just changed. We believe that once your website is set up, there are few things more important than SEO. SEO is how people find out about you—that you exist on the internet. It is important also because of the simple fact that when people use search engines, they usually only look at the top few results. If you are not on the first page of results, it's like you don't exist. The point of SEO is to get your website in those coveted top spots. Relevance and importance matter for ranking. Relevance of the page is determined by keywords in the title tag, keyword use in the body of text, topical relevance of inbound links, duplicate content and tags, and usage data. Importance and credibility are determined by the age of the site, link popularity internally and externally, rate of acquisition of links, and social media.

There are people and companies who do nothing but optimization for a living. In earlier days, optimization could cost quite a bit of money—to the tune of tens of thousands of dollars. But you can go a long way in doing it yourself. You start off with content. What does content consist of? Just adding your social media to your website creates content. The more content the better. In other words: **Content is King**—specifically content quality and accessibility. Creating content that people find interesting is the most "organic" way to move up through search engine rankings. A website must contain useful content that will captivate visitors while satisfying the query they originally searched for.

So, start with content. Now is the time to tie in all of the social media accounts you set up earlier. Of course you've noticed social media icons on websites. Make sure the ones on your website are clickable and go to your social media account.

Your website should link as many as these that are relevant to your business. This is how potential customers are not only going to find you but will also spread the word about your products or services. Customers are spending an increasing amount of time on social media talking about companies, so it is important to take advantage and manage this conversation.

Is there more you can do? Yes, add a blog. There are a number of blog platforms you can use such as blogger.com/start. A blog is important for at least two reasons. First, it increases your visibility on the internet and second, it allows you to communicate with potential and existing customers. The thing about having a blog though, is it must be updated constantly. This also applies to your entire website—update it often. Make it fresh, change content, keep people coming back to see what you are up to. Keep the traffic flowing to your website.

You also want other bloggers to talk about your products or services. There are quite a few bloggers (a gross understatement) out there that can have a huge influence on consumers. If they like your product or services and write a glowing report, you are inevitably going to see an increase in sales and demand.

First motto: Blog and Be Blogged!

Second motto: Update Your Blog and Website Constantly.

Third motto: Link Your Blog to Facebook,

And whatever you do, do not forget or downplay the importance of video content. You want and need video content. More than likely, you have a friend or family member who knows how to create a video and can put one together for you showing off your company and products. If not, try to find a local film student who can help you out. Keep it short and make it fun. Then post it.

Next is **keyword research and targeting**. Simply put, you need to choose keywords that search engine users are likely to use to find your content. An important component of any SEO strategy is to figure out the keywords and optimize your pages with these words. They should be included in the:

- Title (the earlier the better)

- Meta-description (to increase clicks)

- URL (if possible)

- Page headings

- Body of the text

- Related content should be included in the main text.

There are several ways to refine your keywords to get the best results. First you want to see if you can find niche keywords. (see: Reference Sheet for review of best website tools for this).

Next you want to see what keywords your competition is using. There are several websites that show you how to do this; we've provided one on our Reference Sheet from ahrefs.com/blog. As pointed out on this website, you want to do a keyword competitive analysis which is where you determine relevant, valuable keywords that your competitors are ranking well with, but that you are not.

Third, you want to know how competitive your keywords are. Keyword competition refers to how difficult it is for a specific keyword to rank on search engine results pages. See the article on wordstream.com on our Reference Sheet for more information

Once you have your keywording sorted out, you can turn to **link building**. You must create direct link references to content internally on your site and from reputable external sources. A large component of a page's rank will depend on other websites linking to your website. This is called a backlink and may be as important as your content. It is more than "votes" for your site. It establishes your credibility. An important part of any SEO strategy is to get as many inbound links as possible. Remember, not all links are created equal. You want to be linked from recognizable sources such as newspapers, chambers of commerce, or reputable bloggers. Although this is a short paragraph, the importance of backlinking cannot be overstated!

Now your website is up and running. The next step is to go to developers.google.com/search so it will show up on a search. Follow this up with Bing® webmaster tools that can be found at www.bing.com/webmasters/about (yes, the specific links are on our Reference Sheet). These will generate free search engine traffic that may prove vital to your business.

If you want an insight into your internet presence and what is being said about your company, go to www.google.com/alerts and type in the name of your company. Google will keep you up to date on posts about your company. Whether it is good or bad, at least you will know what's being talked about.

☑ Create & Grow Your E-mail List.

A good, high-quality e-mail list is as important as SEO. In fact, if you are selling a product, it may be more important. Consider it your customer list because from this list you will get your buyers and repeat buyers. Why do you think almost every commercial website has a pop-up window offering incentives such as discounts if you enter your e-mail address? You should do the same! In addition, if you have other people working with you, you can ask if they are willing to add their e-mail addresses to your list. Other ideas include having your followers subscribe to your email list so they can receive updates, exclusive content, or special offers. You can create contests or giveaways that require participants to enter with their email addresses. Consider participating in trade shows or events that collect email addresses from interested attendees.

We're sure you can think of other ways, but we repeat, if you are selling products online, **nothing may be more important than this list.** It needs to be constantly updated and grown.

As a note, we believe it is a bad idea to purchase e-mail lists. There are many reasons we think this, including harm to your reputation because using them will come across as spam, many will more than likely be outdated addresses, there may well be legal consequences for privacy violations, and the odds of engagement are poor at best.

- CHAPTER 13 -
LAUNCH IT

☑ Verify You Have the Right Supplier / Manufacturer.

You know your costs, now you need to make sure that you can get the quantities you have projected. As you grow bigger you may find that distributors or even retailers want to make sure you can keep up with their consumer demand. Some retailers may even require that you enter into a Never Out of Stock or NOOS agreement with attendant software that allows them to see your inventory in real time. No company, be it a distributor or retailer, wants to put the time and resources into a brand that cannot fulfill their orders.

☑ Meet with Potential Buyers if Selling Retail.

If you are selling retail, it's time to put your sales rep(s) to work. They need to go out to all potential retailers and let them see what will be coming and get pre-orders. Ideally, they should already have a list of all potential stores in their area or have already put one together from their research, including driving around. Then it is just a matter of visiting each of the stores utilizing all the tools you have created for them including samples, your LookBook, and Line Sheets. Again, the goal here is to get pre-orders.

As an owner you may need to get out there too, particularly if you will be selling through a distributor or broker. At Guzzi Foods® we arranged to meet with several food brokers to get their interest and/or commitment before going into full production. Here is your chance to get real feedback on how others think your products will do in the marketplace. If you can make them as enthusiastic as you are about what you have to offer, and if they sign you up, you know you have something!

☑ Advertise Pre-sales on Your Online Store.

Advertising pre-sales online requires a well-thought-out strategy to generate excitement, build anticipation, and encourage potential customers to make a purchase commitment before the product is officially released. Here's some things you should do:

✓ Create teaser content to build anticipation. Use intriguing visuals, short videos, and captivating copy to generate curiosity about your upcoming product(s).

✓ Utilize your social media platforms to announce and promote the pre-sales. Share teaser content, behind-the-scenes glimpses, and exclusive information to engage your audience. Consider using countdowns to create a sense of urgency.

✓ Use your email list to send out pre-sale announcements. Craft compelling emails that highlight the benefits of pre-ordering, exclusive offers, or limited-time discounts for early buyers.

✓ Design a dedicated landing page on your website specifically for the pre-sale. Clearly communicate the value proposition, features, and benefits of the product. Include visuals and a prominent call-to-action (CTA) for pre-ordering.

✓ Encourage pre-sales by offering exclusive incentives, such as early-bird discounts. Make sure to clearly communicate the added value customers will receive by pre-ordering.

✓ Partner with influencers or industry experts to create buzz around your pre-sales. Influencers can provide authentic reviews, unboxing videos, and testimonials that can reach a broader audience and enhance credibility.

✓ Utilize paid advertising on platforms like Facebook, Instagram, Google Ads, and other relevant channels. Target your ads to reach your specific audience and use compelling visuals and ad copy to highlight the pre-sale benefits.

✓ Make sure your pre-sales campaign is optimized for mobile users, as many people browse and make purchases from their mobile devices.

Once these are in action you need to track the performance of your pre-sales campaign using analytics tools and adjusting your strategy based on the data you gather. By implementing these tactics, you can effectively promote pre-sales online and build a strong foundation for the success of your product launch.

☑Go Into Production on a Small Scale.

Your first run should be on a small scale. The advantages of doing so are quite a few:

- Starting small allows your team to gain experience and learn about the production process, potential challenges, and areas for improvement. This knowledge is invaluable when scaling up production later on.

- Focusing on a smaller quantity initially allows for more meticulous quality control. This can help in identifying and resolving any quality issues before ramping up production, ensuring that your final product meets or exceeds customer expectations.

- Testing the supply chain with a small production run helps identify potential bottlenecks, logistical challenges, or issues with suppliers. This information is valuable in optimizing the production process before scaling up.

- Small-scale production can help maintain better control over cash flow, as the financial outlay is reduced compared to large-scale manufacturing.

So how much should you make? You start with pre-orders from retailers if you are selling to them. If you are strictly online sales, then add up your advertised pre-sales. If you are selling through a distributor or broker, get their opinion. Then you simply sum them all up. You should probably add at least ten percent more for re-orders. At this early stage though, it is pretty much educated guesswork, but by starting small you can avoid a lot of headaches.

☑ Have a Place to Store Your Products.

Okay, now you have run your production. Where are you going to put it? Obviously, you must have a place to store it. A lot is going to depend on the size of your products and quantity of your production. Take jewelry, for instance. That's something you should keep in your possession as opposed to warehousing. If possible, you want to store the products yourself to save on the costs associated with warehousing. This may even mean renting a monthly storage locker. The idea is to initially keep down your costs. Doing your own storing and shipping really helps in this regard.

However, if your product is on the larger size, such as a standup paddle board, and you manufactured quite a few of them, say 500, then you must look at warehousing, also known as 3PL (Third Party Logistics). According to the Council of Supply Chain Management Professionals, 3PL is defined as "a firm that provides multiple logistics services for use by customers. Preferably, these services are integrated, or bundled together, by the provider. Among the services 3PLs provide are transportation, warehousing, cross-docking, inventory management, packaging, and freight forwarding."

Cross-docking refers to the logistics of unloading materials from an incoming semi-trailer truck or railroad car and then loading these materials directly into outbound trucks, trailers, or rail cars, with little or no storage in between.

A 3PL takes all of the problems of storing, shipping, and keeping track of inventory off your hands. Of course, it comes with a cost. Typically, there are at least three costs: cost per piece coming into the warehouse; cost per piece going out of the warehouse; and monthly cost for storing your goods. On top of that you have the trucking costs associated with delivering the products to the warehousing and the shipping cost for getting the products to your retailers.

Let's go over these costs again:

1. If your products are made out of the country, there is usually a charge from the factory to truck the products to the dock or airport you designate.

2. The products are then shipped to the U.S. by boat or plane.

3. A truck then takes them from the port of entry to the warehouse.

4. The warehouse charges a fee for each piece that comes in.

5. The warehouse charges a monthly storage fee for each piece it stores.

6. The warehouse charges a fee for each piece that then goes out.

7. There is a trucking charge to ship the products to the designated retail location, be that the actual store or its warehouse.

Each of these costs have to be accounted for when determining your margins. As you can see, making your products domestically reduces some of these fees. It also eliminates shipping delays such as ships breaking down at sea, products held up by customs, dock worker strikes, etc., all of which we have experienced first-hand. There's a lot to be said for made in the USA!

From past experience we can tell you there is good warehousing and there is really bad warehousing. So go out and visit the site for yourself. See how they handle the products, how they are stored, how they handle returns. See who else is using their service and talk to them. Compare the pricing and range of services. As mentioned in the next section, some 3PLs will also handle the orders from your online store for a separate fee. Also get recommendations. We'll give you one if you are in Southern California—NRI®—highly recommended.

An Important Message about Tariffs:
The Good, the Bad, and the Ugly

At the time of publishing our book, the U.S. business community is experiencing an unprecedented, (actually, not since 1931, when it triggered the Great Recession) anti-business global trade policy. It is on and off again, just sufficiently confusing to disrupt global trade. The import community is the tail on this dog. No matter what the outcome, you as an entrepreneur have to protect your interests. A tariff is simply a fee added to the cost of any imported goods. The importing company must pay the tariffs to the U.S. government prior to the goods clearing customs. The process itself is simple: all cost of goods, plus the tariff in effect at the time of shipping, will equal landed cost. Landed cost, plus your margin, will equal your approximate wholesale. This will have a major impact on your retail. In a standard 50% margin for the importer, and a 50% margin for the retailer, each dollar of additional tariff will cause a $4.00 increase at retail!

What can you do? Actually, not much. You can try to move production to a lower-cost country, but not if you are unsure of the tariff rate there, so that's no solution. As we said earlier, building in China Lake is far more convenient than China!

The good news is that by the time you read this, the issue might be resolved. The bad news is that if it has not been resolved, your retail pricing may be way higher than you expected. The ugly news is how unnecessary this whole experience has been.

Do what the US Marines do: *adapt and overcome!*

☑ Have Your Online Store Ready to Sell.

Your online store can become an excellent source of income. As a matter of policy your online store should charge the same as your retailers. Why? Because you don't want to undercut your retailers and lose their business. If a retailer goes to your online store and sees that you are charging less, you are going to have a very unhappy retailer and a lot of explaining to do.

The good news is that by keeping your online pricing the same as retail, you are getting much higher margins than your wholesale business. In fact, if you are doing your own shipping, your margins can be TRIPLE wholesale. Let's take an example. The cost of your product is $10. Your wholesale price to retailers is $20. So, you make $10. The retailer sells it for $40, so your online store matches this price. Now you are making $30 on each transaction instead of $10.

At some point, however, doing the shipping on your own and handling returns will become too time consuming. It is at that time that you must start using a fulfillment service, whether it is a service to fulfill your online orders or retail orders. While many 3PLs provide this service, there are also smaller operations that just do fulfillment, nothing else.

All are going to take a piece of the action, typically 25%. So, your margin is cut down, but you are still making 50% more than wholesale and have a lot less headaches. Taking the example we used above, while your cost remains the same at $10, you get $30 per transaction rather than $40. The fulfillment center took 25% of $40 or $10, so you are making $20.

It should be noted also that usually the fulfillment center does not charge a separate warehousing fee, so your products, in reasonable quantities, can be stored there free of charge.

☑ Create a Launch Plan and Follow It.

How do you go about this? First, set clear goals and objectives for the launch with deadlines and a budget. By doing this you will know the resources you'll need to allocate to the launch.

If you are selling online, your pre-sale campaign pretty much acted as your launch. But if you are selling strictly brick and mortar, you should take almost the exact same steps as an online pre-sales campaign. You need to create a teaser campaign to generate interest before the launch. Like a trailer for a movie, you want to let people in on what's going to happen without giving away the ranch—remember it is a teaser! The campaign should be developed in a way that allows use for social media, email marketing, and announcements by influencers to build anticipation. This means having marketing materials such as videos, blog posts, brochures, and social media content that has consistent branding and messaging across all materials.

A launch event is all-hands-on-deck. You need to assemble a team responsible for the different aspects of the launch, including marketing, sales, and customer support.

Now you are ready to launch. Be sure to announce the launch date and time well in advance. If your budget can afford it, have a formal launch event. This should be carefully choreographed with media coverage that in turn can be used as marketing material. The launch should include email blasts, social media posts, and online ads. The idea is to disseminate your products as far and wide as possible. Make it informative and fun!

☑ Get Out There and Promote Your Business/Products.

Time to put your marketing plan to work. You want to get your business and product names out as quickly as possible, and by all means possible, that preferably do not break the bank. Remember name recognition is the name of the game.

Online advertising is about as important as it can get. You'll find the link to a good article on this topic on our Reference Sheet: blog.hubsport.com/marketing.

You will probably find that online marketing is going to be where you will be spending most of your advertising budget. So, take the time to read about and understand the various options and strategies before outlaying any cash.

Don't forget the easy marketing ideas such as handing out your business cards, creating stickers that incorporate both your business name and logo, and although a bit more costly, giving away T-shirts or hats. There is nothing like having people walking around with your business or product name. Car dealers know how to do it. I have never seen one that did not have promotional frames for the license plates on every car they sell.

If you are going to sell your products in retail stores, you will need to create POP or Point of Purchase signs—those placards that you see around stores that promote products. Your LookBook photos can easily be converted into POP by simply adding the company and product name.

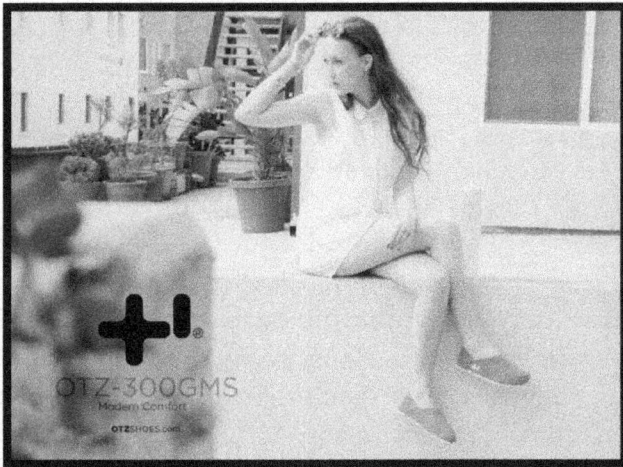

A good company to help you with creating POP is Modernistic (link on our Reference Sheet). Look around—there are probably quite a few others.

Nobody knows your business better than you and you have invested time and energy in your marketing plan, so implement it to the hilt!

☑ Get Products to Your Buyers.

Late shipments can really hurt your business, particularly when you are a young business. Retailers want the product delivered at the times you agreed to when you took their orders. Online customers want their orders even faster. Amazon has spoiled all of us by its lightning-fast deliveries. Although you will probably not be able to match Amazon, you want to get as close as you can.

Here's some things you can do:

✓ Automate your order processing as much as possible to reduce manual errors and save time.

✓ Make sure you have a reliable inventory management system to track product levels in real time.

✓ Work with a warehouse or 3PL who can get your orders out right away.

✓ Consider using multiple fulfillment centers strategically located to reduce shipping times and costs.

✓ Partner with reliable and efficient shipping carriers to ensure timely, cost-effective deliveries.

When it comes to shipping, don't forget to try to negotiate the shipping rates. More than likely, because most companies are currently offering free shipping, you will have to also. Every penny saved by reduced shipping costs is money in your pocket. You'll find a good article on how to go about this linked in our Reference Sheet: goshippo.com.

People love getting the things they ordered in a timely manner. Be sure not to let them down!

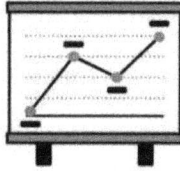

- CHAPTER 14 -
GROW IT

This subject is really a separate book. *And will be in the future.* There is quite a bit of advice out there on how to grow your business. Do an internet or AI search on "how to grow a business" and see for yourself. We are not going to go into great detail here on this subject but want to give you an idea about some of the things you should consider shortly after you launch your business.

☑ Build Momentum.

There are numerous ways to build momentum. Here are some that have been known to work:

1. Clearly define the features and benefits of what you are selling or doing in your POP and brochures.

2. Create loyalty and referral programs.

3. Use special discount coupons on your website for particular people or groups of people.

4. Create new point of purchase (POP) displays for your retail customers each time you ship new product.

5. Have online store holiday discounts.

6. Attend as many trade shows as your budget will permit.

7. Obtain legitimate mailing lists of prospective customers and send out announcements including booth numbers for upcoming tradeshows.

8. Send out yearly holiday cards.

9. Try to get as much media coverage as you can.

10. Hold special events and promote them heavily.

☑ **Arrange for Additional Finance.**

It is almost inevitable that as your company grows, you will need more money. This usually happens because you don't get paid right away. Many retail accounts will demand 60 to 90-day terms to pay you. Then there are returns and mark-downs. You find you have to pay for the next round of production before you have been paid for the last round. You need to pump more money into marketing and advertising to reach higher levels of expansion.

Here's where many a good company has met its ruin. You wouldn't think that too much expansion can cause failure, but we can assure you it can. It's known as out running capital—you don't have enough money to meet your production costs. How does this happen? Because, as we already said, you have not received your money back from an earlier production when you have to pay for the next production.

One of the smartest ways to lock in growth capital is to align with an inventory financing company. These companies offer an option for non-dilutive borrowing, meaning that you do not have to give up equity to obtain growth capital. It is cheaper to finance inventory and grow your company while retaining your equity. Imagine the difference if you gave up 25% of your company to buy inventory, and with the funds, grew your company by 50%. Looks good. But you gave up 25% of your ownership to grow. Now let's suppose you retained your equity, borrowed the same amount, and experienced the same growth. 100% of the profit is yours because you did not give up equity. This one simple action can be a very significant wealth builder. Imagine that this loan generated successive 100% growth for three years. See the difference in the value of retaining your equity? Another example of an inventory financer we know is Beacons Capital.com. Check their webpage for more details. . . AND RETAIN YOUR EQUITY!

So, you have to plan your expansion on the amount of capital you have or know you can get.

☑ Understand the Importance of Credit Granting Practices.

As a seller of a product, there may come a time when you will have to extend credit to get your product to market. This is particularly true if you are selling to a retail store or business. Before extending credit, carefully analyze the financial stability and creditworthiness of potential retail customers. It's crucial to strike a balance between promoting sales growth and managing the risks associated with credit transactions. Regularly reassess your credit policies and make adjustments as your business and customer base evolve.

Here are some considerations and steps to take if you are thinking about extending credit to retail stores:

1. **Assess the Risks & Benefits:** The potential benefits of extending credit to retail stores include increased sales and business relationships. However, you also need to consider the risks, including the possibility of late or non-payment and the impact on your cash flow.

2. **Credit Application Process:** Require retail stores to complete a credit application that provides essential information about the store's financial health and business history. Also don't forget to check credit references.

3. **Set Credit Limits:** Establish credit limits for each retail store based on their financial stability and creditworthiness. This can help mitigate the risk of large unpaid invoices which we have found by experience to be quite painful.

4. **Terms & Conditions:** Clearly outline the terms and conditions of the credit agreement. This includes payment terms (e.g., net 30 days), interest rates on overdue payments, and any penalties for late payments.

5. **Collection Policy:** Develop a clear and effective collections policy for dealing with overdue payments. Establish a systematic approach to follow up on late payments, including sending reminders and pursuing legal action only if necessary.

One excellent way to granting retail terms is to work with a factoring company. It is a very common practice. In essence, a factor buys your order from you for a specific retailer, and in exchange, guarantees payment to you. They charge a fee, but again, the payment is guaranteed. This is an excellent opportunity to reduce risk and make your money go further. There are many options online and you can also ask any good retailer if they can recommend a good factor.

Fostering positive relationships with retail stores by using good communication and understanding their business needs will help you build a successful retail presence which can be quite lucrative.

☑ Carry Adequate Inventory.

Some people in business think it sounds good when you tell a distributor or retailer that you are all sold out of one or more of your products because it shows demand. They are right in that it does show demand but fail to see that if they had more inventory, they would have had more sales. As a startup you don't want to run out of product. At the early stage of any business, every sale is important. Every sale means more solvency. The idea is to make money. This is only going to happen if you have products to sell. This even applies to services. If you are so overwhelmed by demand for your services and can't take on another client who wants your services, it's probably time to do some hiring.

In the land of products though, the way to meet increased demand is by having adequate inventory. The trick is not to have too little or too much. So how do you know how much to carry?

Believe it or not, there is actually a formula to determine the optimal order quantity that minimizes the total inventory costs. It is called the economic order quantity (EOQ) and it takes into account the costs associated with ordering and holding inventory.

Here is the basic formula:

$$EOQ = \sqrt{\frac{2DS}{H}}$$

Where:

Demand (D):

D is the total number of units you expect to sell or use in a given period (typically a year). Use historical sales data or sales forecasts to estimate demand.

Ordering Cost per Order (S):

S represents the cost of placing an order. It includes costs such as processing, paperwork, shipping, and any other costs associated with placing and receiving an order.

Holding Cost per Unit per Year (H):

H is the cost of holding one unit of inventory for a year. It includes costs such as storage, insurance, and the opportunity cost of tying up capital in inventory.

Once you have the values of D, S, and H, plug them into the EOQ formula to calculate the optimal order quantity. The square root is used because the EOQ formula is derived from the trade-off between ordering costs and holding costs, and the square root helps find the minimum point of the total cost curve.

It's important to note that while the EOQ provides a useful starting point, real-world situations may involve additional complexities, such as fluctuating demand, variable ordering costs, or limited storage space.

Okay, if you can figure that out, more power to you! For those of us who are less mathematically inclined the key metrics are sales history and pre-sales if you are selling to retail. Your sales history should be graphed so you can see how your sales are performing and which direction they are heading (hopefully always up). If you see continuous growth of ten percent, then you know to add at least ten percent more than your last order. If you are selling multiple products, each should be separately graphed so you can weed out or put more marketing toward the under performers. But if one model is outperforming others, then you know to order more than before. You want to ride the winner!

If you have pre-sales, they may be the best indicator, but you should add to that amount to account for unforeseen events or fluctuations in demand by maintaining a safety stock. This extra stock can prevent sellouts and fulfil unexpected orders.

☑ Expand Your Trademarks.

Are you ready to expand into markets in other countries? Here's where international markets come into consideration. There are some huge markets out there, particularly in Asia, such as South Korea and China, not to mention Japan and the Philippines.

There are a number of companies that help you get trademarks in other countries, including Marcaria® and Trademarkia®, discussed earlier.

Trademark knockoff in other countries is common practice. The United States Patent & Trademark Office (USPTO) published an excellent article that discusses this. You will find the link to the entire article on our Reference Sheet, which we encourage you to read. What follows is the introduction:

Don't Sit and Wait: Stopping Trademark Squatters

"Here's a scary situation. Let's say you manufacture or sell your product outside the United States, or you plan to in the future. Things are going well. Orders are steady, interest is widespread, and you see demand in other markets. When you're ready to expand into one of those markets, you discover someone else has already registered your trademark there. Not only can you not register your own brand, the current owner may now actually control your ability to manufacture and sell your product in that country.

Unfortunately, many U.S. companies have confronted situations like this over the years. It's a practice known as "bad-faith trademark filing"—sometimes referred to as "trademark squatting."

Information curtesy USPTO

The moral of the story is to obtain the trademarks for all other countries you think you will be doing business in at the earliest opportunity, particularly China. You do not want to be the victim of a trademark squatter.

☑ Know the Importance of Customer Service.

We can't say enough about the importance of GOOD customer service! Customer service can make or break a company. A good viewpoint to have is to go beyond your customers' expectations. And above all don't complain about returns; we favor generous return policies.

It has been said that it can cost seven times more to acquire a new customer than to retain an existing one, so making customer service a priority is just good business practice. Create a social media presence and start a blog on your site so that customers have a way to communicate and feel heard. Conduct occasional surveys and ask for customer feedback and testimonials to understand the strengths and weaknesses of your customer service. When your customers feel heard and cared for, they'll keep coming back.

A good customer service rep is worth their weight in gold!

☑ Keep Getting Professional Advice.

In Chapter One we discussed the different programs available to seek advice on starting your business. If you used any of them, then you know they are also there to help you grow. So, use them.

But now that your business has been launched, there is one additional program we would like to bring to your attention—"10,000 Small Businesses," sponsored by Goldman Sachs®:

> Big Ideas/Big Network/Big Impact: Goldman Sacks 10,000 Small Businesses is an investment in the growth of small businesses. We help entrepreneurs create jobs and economic opportunity by providing access to education, capital, and

support services.

Goldman Sachs *10,000 Small Businesses* is designed to tap into that economic power by providing entrepreneurs across the country with the resources they need to grow and create jobs.

The program is currently operating in Chicago, Cleveland, Detroit, Houston, Long Beach, Los Angeles, Miami, New Orleans, New York, Philadelphia, and Salt Lake City. It will continue to expand on a city-by-city basis.

Online videos are another source. You'll find one we recommend on our Reference Sheet.

Keep getting advice from those who have been "there." It may well make all the difference!

CONCLUSION

Thank you for reading our book. We created this guide because we did not have one when we started our businesses. The biggest error is always the one you made because you were uninformed!

There is really nothing quite like creating and owning your own business. You will probably have a good number of sleepless nights, but if you can make a go of it, it will be worth it.

We hope this book helps you reach your dreams!

Stay in touch with us at our website:

www.aftertheidea.com

APPENDIX A
REFERENCE SHEET

To access the Reference Sheet containing live links to the websites referred to in this book, use this QR code:

APPENDIX B
SWOT ANALYSIS

Strengths, Weaknesses, Opportunities and Threats…
Be honest, take a deep breath, make a chart.
Day 1 at OTZShoes Chart:

STRENGTHS

- Great product story

- Unique shape & appearance

- Very affluent global LOHAS (lifestyle of health & sustainability)

- Unique positioning between comfort & fashion

- Cork footbeds

WEAKNESSES

- Startup

- Weak financing

- No backroom, accounting platform

- Distribution

- No sales team

- High cost, low volume manufacturer

- High price/low margins

OPPORTUNITIES

- U.S. market 5,000 comfort retailers

- Global LOHAS consumer

- Large e-commerce possibilities (Zappos)

- Large in-house e-commerce possibilities

- "Sleepy" traditional comfort market

THREATS

- Large market too hard to approach

- Established brands dominating retail

- Unprepared to deliver service

- Small factory, low quality, high prices

- Limited marketing budget

It hurt us to lay out the weaknesses, but we did. The long-term solution was of course to address the weaknesses and turn as many around as we could. In essence, make our weaknesses less weak, possibly stronger. We shifted factories, added a public logistics company, added an IT platform, and found more operating capital. Look at the new SWOT analysis done at the end of year 2: Day 720 OTZShoes Chart:

STRENGTHS

- Great product story

- Unique shape & appearance

- Very affluent global LOHAS (lifestyle of health & sustainability)

- Unique positioning between comfort & fashion

- Cork footbeds

WEAKNESSES

- No global marketing budget

- Low volume boutique manufacturing

- No global SEO funding

- No global sales team

STRENGTHS

- Great product story

- Unique shape & appearance

- Very affluent global LOHAS (lifestyle of health & sustainability)

- Unique positioning between comfort & fashion

- Cork footbeds

WEAKNESSES

- No global marketing budget

- Low volume boutique manufacturing

- No global SEO funding

- No global sales team

APPENDIX C
MUTUAL CONFIDENTIALITY AND
NON-DISCLOSURE AGREEMENT

This Agreement effective this _____ day of _____ 202_, is by and between_____. ("AA"), and_____("BB").

RECITALS

WHEREAS AA and BB are considering a business relationship relating to the research and development of the formulation and processing of GF's yogurt-based aerosol ("the Project"); and

WHEREAS it may be necessary for the parties to disclose to each other certain valuable confidential and proprietary information, including formulations, costs, and manufacturing procedures and processes; and

WHEREAS, the parties recognize that the information to be disclosed by the other party during the Project is the confidential, proprietary, and trade secret information of the other party, and that the disclosure of such information (individually and collectively referred to herein as the "Confidential Information") is made only with the understanding that the party receiving the information will maintain the confidentiality of the Confidential Information as herein provided and that such information shall be used only for the purposes of completing the Project.

AGREEMENT

NOW THEREFORE, the parties for good and valuable consideration, the receipt and sufficiency of which are hereby acknowledged, hereto agree as follows:

1. DESCRIPTION OF CONFIDENTIAL INFORMATION. Any and all Confidential Information disclosed by either party, which by its nature is generally considered proprietary and confidential, shall be considered

Confidential Information, including designs, use, materials, product formulas, manufacturing processes and procedures, ingredient information, cost and financial data, or other information not generally known by third parties.

2. AGREEMENT TO MAINTAIN CONFIDENTIALITY. Both parties agree to hold any Confidential Information disclosed by the other party during the Project in strict confidence during and after the termination of the Project and this Agreement; provided, however, that neither party shall incur any liability for (a) disclosure of information which was authorized in writing by an officer of the other party, or (b) is within the public domain or comes within the public domain without any breach of this Agreement, or (c) was in the receiving party's possession prior to disclosure, or (d) is independently developed by the receiving party's employees or agents who have not had access to the Confidential Information, or (e) is required to be disclosed by the receiving party pursuant to judicial order or other compulsion of law, provided that the receiving party shall provide to the other party prompt notice of such order.

All notes, memoranda, reports, drawings, manuals, records, papers, data, and other written materials of every kind relating to the Project or to the business of either party which are provided to the receiving party at any time during the term of this Agreement containing any such Confidential Information shall be the sole and exclusive property of the party providing the information. Upon the written request of either party, the receiving party shall surrender this property, and any copies or excerpts thereof, to the other party.

3. LIMITED DISCLOSURE. The disclosure of Confidential Information by either party shall be made only to agents or employees of that party who have a need-to-know. Both parties agree to inform any such agents or employees of the existence of this Agreement and will instruct them to treat as confidential and preserve the confidentiality of the Confidential Information pursuant to this Agreement.

4. USE OF CONFIDENTIAL INFORMATION. Both parties agree that they shall not use any Confidential Information for any purpose other than to complete the work on the Project.

5.   EQUITABLE REMEDIES. Both parties acknowledge that damages would be an inadequate remedy for a breach of this Agreement and that the other party shall be entitled to enforce this Agreement by any action for specific performance or for injunctive relief, or both, to prevent the breach or continued breach of this Agreement.

6.   EFFECTIVE DATE AND LENGTH OF OBLIGATION. This Agreement is effective as of the date first written above and may be terminated by either party at any time upon written notice. The obligations of confidentiality and non-use for Confidential Information hereunder shall continue beyond the termination of this Agreement.

7.   GOVERNING LAW. This Agreement shall be governed by and construed in accordance with the laws of the State of _____, without reference to conflicts of law principles. The parties hereby submit and consent to the jurisdiction of the federal and state courts of the State of _____ for purposes of any legal action arising out of this Agreement.

IN WITNESS WHEREOF, the parties have executed this Agreement as of the date first above written.

Name: _____

Date: _____

Name: _____

Date: _____

APPENDIX D
Example Line Sheet

VIBΛ®

Date:

Company Name:

Bill To:

Ship To:

PO#:

Start Ship:

Cancel Date:

Shipping account #:

SS 2025

Name	Color	Code	35	36	37	38	39	40	41	42	43	44	45	46	47	48	Total	Wholesale	Total Price	Retail
PORTO Bio Leather	Desert Nude	PORTOBLDNG																72.50		145.00
PORTO Bio Leather	Preto Black	PORTOBLPBB																72.50		145.00
ZUMA Linen	Agave Blue	ZUMAVLABG																72.50		145.00
ZUMA Linen	Beachpebble Grey	ZUMAVLBGG																72.50		145.00
ZUMA Linen	Constellation Black	ZUMAVLCBG																72.50		145.00
ZUMA Linen	Oak Brown	ZUMAVLOBG																72.50		145.00
ZUMA Linen	Pacific Blue	ZUMAVLPBG																72.50		145.00
ZUMA Linen	Pomegranate Red	ZUMAVLPRG																72.50		145.00
ZUMA Linen	Sagebrush Green	ZUMAVLSGG																72.50		145.00
ZUMA Linen	Sand Dollar	ZUMAVLSDG																72.50		145.00
ZUMA Linen	Wild Rose	ZUMAVLWRG																72.50		145.00
SAINT TROPEZ Leather	Cocoa Brown	STROPEZRLCOBB																87.50		175.00
SAINT TROPEZ Leather	Cognac Brown	STROPEZRLCGBG																87.50		175.00
SAINT TROPEZ Leather	Fawn Tan	STROPEZRLFTG																87.50		175.00
SAINT TROPEZ Leather	Preto Black	STROPEZRLPBB																87.50		175.00
AMALFI Leather	Cognac Brown	AMALFIRLCGBG																97.50		195.00
AMALFI Leather	Preto Black	AMALFIRLPBB																97.50		195.00
CAPRI Leather	Cognac Brown	CAPRIRLCGBG																102.50		205.00
CAPRI Leather	Preto Black	CAPRIRLPBB																102.50		205.00
ROMA Leather	Cocoa Brown	ROMARLCOBB																87.50		175.00
ROMA Leather	Cognac Brown	ROMARLCGBG																87.50		175.00
ROMA Leather	Fawn Tan	ROMARLFTG																87.50		175.00
ROMA Leather	Preto Black	ROMARLPBB																87.50		175.00
ROMA Leather	Sunflower Yellow	ROMARLSYG																0.00		
ROMA WOVEN Leather	Cognac Brown	ROMAWRLCGBG																122.50		245.00
ROMA WOVEN Leather	Preto Black	ROMAWRLPBB																122.50		245.00
ROMA Wool	1956 Laranja	ROMAW1956L																82.50		165.00
ROMA Wool	1956 Bege	ROMAW1956B																82.50		165.00
ROMA Wool	Chestnut Brown	ROMAWCB																82.50		165.00
ROMA Wool	Oliva Verde	ROMAWOV																82.50		165.00
ROMA Wool	Heather Grey	ROMAWHG																82.50		165.00
ROMA Wool	Fez Yellow	ROMAWFY																82.50		165.00
ZUMA Leather	Cocoa Brown	ZUMARLCOBB																97.50		195.00
ZUMA Leather	Cognac Brown	ZUMARLCGBG																97.50		195.00
ZUMA Leather	Preto Black	ZUMARLPBB																97.50		195.00
JTREE Bio Suede	Constellation Black	JTREEBSCBB																117.50		235.00
JTREE Bio Suede	Desert Sand	JTREEBSDSG																117.50		235.00
HELSINKI Leather	Cocoa Brown	HELRLCOBB																122.50		245.00
HELSINKI Leather	Cognac Brown	HELRLCGBG																122.50		245.00
HELSINKI Leather	Preto Black	HELRLPBB																122.50		245.00
TOTAL																					

Kids

Name	Color	Code	28	29	30	31	32	33	34										Wholesale	Total Price	Retail
ZUMA Linen Kids	Agave Blue	ZUMAVLKABH																57.50		115.00
ZUMA Linen Kids	Oak Brown	ZUMAVLKOBC																57.50		115.00
ZUMA Linen Kids	Plum Pink	ZUMAVLKPPH																57.50		115.00
ZUMA Linen Kids	Sand Dollar	ZUMAVLKSDH																57.50		115.00
TOTAL																					

edited on January 1st, 2025

VIBAe USA Inc. 29910 Cuthbert RD Malibu CA 90265 // Contact info: Ludovic Malmoux Cell: +1 (818) 458 2861

APPENDIX E
Example Chart of Accounts

A1		fx	Category			

	A	B	C	D	E	F	G
1	Category	Account #	Account Name				
2	Assets	1000	Cash - Operating Account				
3	Assets	1010	Petty Cash				
4	Assets	1100	Accounts Receivable				
5	Assets	1200	Inventory - Raw Materials				
6	Assets	1210	Inventory - Finished Goods				
7	Assets	1300	Prepaid Expenses				
8	Assets	1400	Equipment				
9	Assets	1500	Accumulated Depreciation				
10	Liabilities	2000	Accounts Payable				
11	Liabilities	2100	Credit Card Payable				
12	Liabilities	2200	Sales Tax Payable				
13	Liabilities	2300	Loan Payable - SBA				
14	Liabilities	2400	Payroll Liabilities				
15	Equity	3000	Owner's Capital				
16	Equity	3100	Owner's Draw				
17	Equity	3200	Retained Earnings				
18	Revenue	4000	Product Sales - Wholesale				
19	Revenue	4010	Product Sales - Retail				
20	Revenue	4100	R&D Contract Revenue				
21	Revenue	4200	Other Income				
22	Expenses	5000	Cost of Goods Sold				
23	Expenses	5100	Raw Materials				
24	Expenses	5200	Packaging Supplies				
25	Expenses	5300	Rent				
26	Expenses	5400	Utilities				
27	Expenses	5500	Salaries & Wages				
28	Expenses	5600	Payroll Taxes				
29	Expenses	5700	Marketing & Advertising				
30	Expenses	5800	Research & Development				
31	Expenses	5900	Insurance				
32	Expenses	6000	Professional Services				
33	Expenses	6100	Depreciation Expense				
34	Expenses	6200	Travel & Meals				
35	Expenses	6300	Bank & Credit Fees				
36